# Poems of Sophia

# POEMS OF SOPHIA

BY

## ALEXANDER BLOK

*Translated and Edited*
*by*

BORIS JAKIM

First published in the USA
by Semantron Press
© Boris Jakim 2014

Semantron Press is an imprint of
Angelico Press

For information, address:
Angelico Press, Ltd.
4709 Briar Knoll Dr. Kettering, OH 45429
www.angelicopress.com


978-1-62138-066-5

Cover image: detail from *Walk at Dusk*
(*Man Contemplating a Megalith*),
by Caspar David Friedrich, between 1830 and 1835.
Cover design: Michael Schrauzer

# CONTENTS

# Translator's Introduction

## I

"I enter dark temples
And celebrate a poor rite.
I await there the Beautiful Lady
In the glow of red lamps...

O Holy One, how tender are the candles,
How comforting Your features!
I hear neither sighs nor words
But I believe: You are the Dear one."[1]

"I believe in the Sun of the Testament,
I see dawns in the distance.
I await universal light
From the springtime earth...

I pass through forests
Of forbidden lilies.
Angels' wings fill
The heavens above me...

Streams of unfathomable
Light tremble.
I believe in the Sun of the Testament,
I see Your eyes."[2]

1  See p. 131 of the present edition.
2  See p. 94 of the present edition.

[1]

"Before You is the endless blue
Of seas, fields, mountains, and woods;
Birds call to one another in the unbounded heights;
The mist rises, the heavens redden.

And here below, in the dust, in the nothingness,
Having glimpsed for an instant Your immortal features,
A negligible slave, full of inspiration,
I sing You…"[3]

IT WAS THUS that Sophia, the Beautiful Lady, appeared to Alexander Blok at the end of the nineteenth century and the beginning of the twentieth. Blok's early lyrical outpourings (1898–1903) are dominated by this radiant feminine vision with an unearthly countenance, whom he addresses by the capitalized pronoun "You."

Blok identifies his vision with a real girl, Liubov Dmitrievna Mendeleeva, and conducts an ardent courtship of her, both in verse and in the natural landscapes of Shakhmatovo (his grandfather's country estate near Moscow) and Petersburg. He saw and sang the Beautiful Lady in the woods and meadows of Shakhmatovo as well as in the misty, murky maritime setting of Petersburg; he saw Her in the sky over Shakhmatovo and Petersburg as well as in the flowers and birds of Shakhmatovo.

At this time Blok begins to read Vladimir Solovyov, the great poet of Sophia, the mysterious feminine principle behind all creation. Solovyov becomes Blok's guide through the mysterious land of his visions: "…beyond the mists one has a sweet/Presentiment of the coming dawn./For me this all-encompassing poet/Represents the unriddling of the world."[4]

To his verse of 1898–1900 Blok gave the name *"Ante Lucem,"* "before the light (or dawn)," that is, before he saw Her. The pre-dawn period of his life comes to an end; he begins to see amazing dawns: "I was walking toward bliss. My path was shining/With the red light of the evening

---

3  See p. 59 of the present edition.
4  As quoted in Orlov, Vladimir: Zhizn' Bloka: Gamaun, ptitsa veshchaya (The life of Blok: Gamaun, the prophetic bird), Moscow, 2001, p. 84.

dew,/And in my heart a tremulous distant voice/Sang a song of dawn."[5] The spring of 1901 was a mystical turning point for him: He wandered endlessly all over Petersburg, and in his wanderings, "She"— the Mysterious Maiden, the Empress of the Universe, the Eternal Bride—began to appear to him. His visions of Her became embodied in the *Verses about the Beautiful Lady.* The real image of the girl he loved— his fiancée, Liubov[6]—was idealized, merging with the image of the Eternal Feminine. Earthly love was imagined in its absolute and pure beauty. These poems are a diary of his love, describing the romance of a Poet and a Maiden, of a Knight and his Lady, though not in medieval times but in a Russian countryside setting and on a background of turn-of-the-century manorial life. The heroine of the poems lives on a high hill surrounded by jagged woods, and the hero circles the area on a white horse: "Today You were walking alone/And I did not see Your wonders./Above Your high hill/Stretched jagged woods."[7] Though Blok seems to be addressing the Eternal Maiden, he can also be seen as addressing Liubov, who was staying on her father's country estate on a hill separated from Shakhmatovo by a wall of woods. These visions were crowned by the real marriage of the Poet and the Beautiful Lady.[8]

## II

ALEXANDER BLOK (1880–1921) is the greatest Russian poet after Pushkin and perhaps the greatest poet of the 20th century in any language. In his later poems (after 1904) he is a poet of romantic love, of Russia, and of revolution. In his early verse (1898–1904) he is primarily a mystical poet of great lyrical gifts.

Growing up, Blok spent his summers at his grandfather's[9] rustic family manor, Shakhmatovo, outside Moscow. A short distance from Shakh-

---

5 See p. 13 of the present edition.

6 Significantly, "liubov" means "love" in Russian.

7 See p. 56 of the present edition

8 Blok married Liubov on 17 August 1903.

9 Blok's maternal grandfather, Andrei Nikolaevich Beketov (1825–1902), was Russia's greatest botanist. "He and I would roam for hours through woods and swamps. . . . I remember how we rejoiced when we once found . . . a tiny fern: even now, many years

matovo was Boblovo, a manor belonging to the world-famous scientist Dmitry Mendeleev, who was his grandfather's old friend. It was at Boblovo in 1898 that Blok became close to Mendeleev's daughter, Liubov Dmitrievna Mendeleeva, who was to become his wife and the most important person in his life. The highlight of that summer was a performance of *Hamlet* in Boblovo staged by Blok, where he played the Dane and Liubov played Ophelia. After the performance, Blok and Liubov took a midnight stroll and saw a shooting star falling to earth: it was as if an electric current had passed between them.

Blok was one of the great symbolists. Russian symbolism was a way for artists to be co-creators of the world with God. The symbolists would reach into the cosmos and into the human soul, and find bridges between eternity and humanity. The poem, painting, or musical composition becomes an act that creates a new heaven and a new earth. Sophia, the eternal mother and bride, is such bridge. The sky is Her symbol and falling stars connect Her and earth.

THIS VOLUME consists of translations of three collections of Blok's verse—*Ante Lucem* (1898–1900), *Verses about the Beautiful Lady* (1901–1902), and *Crossroads* (1902–1904). The Russian texts that I have used are those published in Volume One of Blok's Collected Works (*Sobranie sochinenii*) in Eight Volumes, edited by V.N. Orlov, A.A. Surkov, and K.I. Chukovsky, Moscow-Leningrad, 1960. Individual poems are numbered and separated by this symbol (  ).

I have made no attempt to reproduce Blok's rhymes; I have made every attempt to reproduce the music and imagery. All the notes to the poems are by the translator.

BORIS JAKIM

---

later [in 1915], I keep going back to that mountain to look for the fern, but haven't been able to find it. . . ." (See Blok's "Avtobiografiya" in vol. 5, Collected Works in Six Volumes, Leningrad, 1982, p. 68.)

# *Ante Lucem*[1]

## (1898–1900)

### PETERSBURG—SHAKHMATOVO

The moon may shine but the night is dark.
Life may bring people happiness
But in my soul the spring of love
Cannot expel the stormy grayness.
The night stretches above me
And responds with a dead glance
To the lusterless gaze of my sick soul,
Drenched in sweet and acrid poison.
And in vain, concealing my passions,
Do I wander among the crowd
In the cold pre-dawn darkness
With a single hidden thought:
The moon may shine but the night is dark.
Life may bring people happiness
But in my soul the spring of love
Will not expel the stormy grayness.
(*January 1898, Petersburg*)

### *To N. Gun*[2]

You've lived much while I've preferred to sing…
You've experienced both life and sorrow,
While to me an invisible spirit has flown down,

1 "Before the light (i.e., dawn)."
2 Nikolai Gun was a high-school friend of Blok.

Opening a sea of powerful sounds...
Your soul is already enchained:
It has been touched by violent storms.
But my soul is free: like fine dust
It is blown by the wind in the azure.

My friend, I have long felt
That life will soon touch me...
But my heart is buried in the earth
And will never spring back to life!

When we grow weary on our path
And are engulfed in the murk of fog,
Come to me then to rest
And I will come to you, my cherished friend!
(*Spring, 1898*)

The full moon has risen over the meadow,
Silently shining with its
Unchanging marvelous circle.
Pale, pale is the flowering meadow
And the nocturnal darkness creeping over it
Rests and sleeps.
Fear keeps you from setting out on the road:
An incomprehensible anxiety
Reigns under the moon,
Though you know that in the early morning
The sun will come out of the mist
And illuminate the meadow,
And then you will take a path
Where life seethes
Under every leaf of grass.
(*21 July 1898, Shakhmatovo*)

### To My Mother

My friend, observe how in the plain of heaven
Smoky little clouds sail under the moon.
Do you see how its pale soulless empty light
Cuts through the immaterial ether?

Enough gazing into this starry sea,
Enough striving toward the cold moon!
Is there insufficient joy in the spaces of everyday life?
Is there insufficient heat in the heart's fire?

The cold moon will not answer you,
There is no strength to reach the distant stars...
The cold of the grave will greet you everywhere
In the distant land of the comfortless orbs...
(*July 1898*)

She was young and beautiful
And has remained a pure Madonna,
Luminous like the mirror of a tranquil stream.
How my heart ached!...

She seemed as carefree as the blue
Distances, as a sleeping swan;
Who knows, perhaps there was also sorrow...
How my heart ached!...

When she sang to me about love,
Her song found a response in my soul,
But the ardent blood did not know passion...
How my heart ached!...
(*27 July 1898*)

*There was only one flower there,*
*Aromatic, incomparable...*
Zhukovsky[3]

I aspire to lavish freedom
And hasten to a beautiful place
Where in a broad pure meadow
Things are as good as in a marvelous dream.
Sumptuous clover grows there
As well as the innocent cornflower
And you always hear the light rustling
Of ears of wheat... There is a long way to go!
There is only one in this whole ocean,
There is only one in all this grass...
You can't see it there, in the mist,
But I saw it—and will pluck it!
(*7 August 1898*)

### 7

Wearied by daytime wanderings,
I sometimes leave all this vanity behind
To remember the wounds of those sufferings,
To churn up the former dreams...

If I could only breathe into her soul
Spring joy on a winter day!
But, no, why, oh why, should I destroy
Her childish ease?

It is enough for my soul to soar
Up to her heavenly heights,
Where we sometimes have a glimpse of joy
Though it is meant—not for us.
(*30 October 1898*)

3  The quotation, taken from Zhukovsky's poem "A Song," is not precise.

In the wild grove by the ravine
There is a green hill in perpetual shadow.
Nearby a stream's living flow
Induces a lazy ease with its gurgling.
Flowers and grasses cover
The green hill and never
Do rays of light penetrate there;
Only the water flows gently.
Lovers, hiding, do not
Gaze into the cool darkness.
Should I tell you why the flowers do not fade
And the source does not dry up?
There, there, deep beneath the roots,
Lie my sufferings,
Nourishing with eternal tears,
Ophelia, your flowers!
(*3 November 1898*)

＊＊9＊＊
*I dreamt that you had died.*
Heine

I dreamt of the death of a beloved person:
High, all in flowers, was placed the somber coffin;
People crowded round and speeches of compassion
Were whispered to me by everyone
While I looked round indifferently and without a thought in my head,
Regarding haughtily those who wished to help me;
I felt that up above was unshakable happiness
While all around me was pitiless night.
I thanked them all for their words of consolation
And pressed their hands, while in my blood sang the thought:
"The blessed, eternal spirit has taken away your suffering!
Blessed is he who has lost a beloved person!"
(*10 November 1898*)

≈≈≈10≈≈≈

*To K. M. S.*[4]

The moon has awakened. The noisy city
Roars in the distance and is afire with its lights.
It is so quiet here but so crazy there,
Everything rings and reverberates there but, here, we are
  alone...
But if the flame of our encounter
Were an eternal and holy flame,
Our conversation would not pour forth as it does,
Your voice would not sound as it does!...
Can it be that suffering still lives
And can steal our happiness?
"At the hour of our indifferent encounter
We will remember the sad farewell..."[5]
(*14 December 1898*)

≈≈≈11≈≈≈

I again dreamt of you[6] in flowers on the noisy stage.
You were crazy like passion and tranquil like a dream
And I, subjugated, bent down before you
And thought: "This is happiness; I am enslaved again!"
But you, Ophelia, gazed at Hamlet
Without happiness, without love, goddess of beauty,
While roses sprinkled on the poor poet
And together with the roses his dreams poured forth, poured forth...
You died, all in a glow of roses,
With flowers on your breast, with flowers on your curls,
While I stood in your fragrance
With flowers on my breast, on my head, in my hands...
(*23 December 1898*)

4  Kseniya Mikhailovna Sadovskaya (1862–1925), an older woman who was Blok's
first love.
5  Lines from Yakov Polonsky's poem "Farewell."
6  Liubov Dmitrievna Mendeleeva, who played Ophelia in Blok's domestic produc-
tion of *Hamlet*. Blok played Hamlet.

At the edge of the heavens is the omega star,
All sparkling, colorful Sirius.
Above my head the mute Vega
Out of the realm of darkness and snow
Has turned to ice above the earth.

In the same way, you, cold goddess,
Reign and wield power
Over my eternally fiery soul
Just as you, cold holiness, reign
Over the eternally fiery star!
(*27 January 1899*)

Dear friend! With your young soul
    You are so pure!
Sleep for now! My soul is with you,
    My beauty!
When you awaken, it will be night and a cold blizzard
    Will be howling.
You will not be alone then but together with your trustworthy
    Friend's soul.
It may be winter all around with its roaring winds
    But I am with you!
Your friend will shelter you from the winter storms
    With all his soul!
(*8 February 1899*)

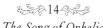
*The Song of Ophelia*

Parting from your dear maid,
My friend, you swore you'd love me!...

Going off into the hateful land
You promised to keep your vow!...

There, beyond happy Denmark,
Your shores are in darkness...
Angry talkative billows
Wash the tears on the cliff...

My dear warrior will not return,
Dressed all in silver...
In the grave the bow and black feather
Will heave painfully...
(*8 February 1899*)

 15

*To good and evil shamefully indifferent,*
*At the onset of our careers we wither if there is no struggle.*
Lermontov[7]

When the crowd around me applauds all sorts of idols,
Toppling some, erecting others,
For blind me there glows somewhere
A holy flame and youth's dawn!
Toward it I strive with my sickly soul,
Strive and aspire to the extent of my powers...
But it seems that with my heavy anguish
I have sunk the ship of hope!
Sucked into an abyss where my heart perishes,
I am a gray indifferent misanthrope...
The crowd shouts—but I am infinitely cold.
The crowd calls—but I am mute and motionless.
(*13 February 1899*)

7  From Lermontov's poem "Thought."

## ༷༷16༷༷

### *Gamaun, the Prophetic Bird*
(after Vasnetsov's painting)[8]

Over the smooth surfaces of endless waters,
Clothed in purple by the sunset,
She prophesies and sings,
Not having the strength to lift her damaged wings…
She prophesies about the cruel Tatar yoke,
She prophesies about a series of bloody executions,
About plague, famine, and fire,
About the power of villains and the downfall of the righteous…
Overwhelmed by a pre-eternal terror,
Her beautiful face shines with love
But prophetic truth issues forth
From her blood-encrusted lips!…
(*23 February 1899*)

## ༷༷17༷༷

I was walking toward bliss. My path was shining
With the red light of the evening dew,
And in my heart a tremulous distant voice
Sang a song of dawn. It sang
A dawn song as the sunset was fading,
The stars were glowing,
And the high seas of the sky
Were burning with the evening purple!…
My soul was burning and my voice was singing
Of the dawn at the evening hour.
I was walking toward bliss. My path was shining
With the red light of the evening dew.
(*18 May 1899*)

8  This poem was inspired by V.M. Vasnetsov's painting of Gamaun, a prophetic bird of paradise of Russian folklore.

Fate itself ordained that I
Shine my dim torch with
Holy veneration
At the very threshold of the Ideal.
And as soon as evening comes, toward the Good
I strive with my earthly mind
And full of unearthly fear
I burn with Poetry's fire.

(*26 May 1899*)

I am old of soul. My long path is some sort of
    Black lot.
A heavy dream, accursed and obstinate,
    Presses on my chest.
So few years but so many terrible thoughts!
    The ailment is heavy…
Save me from obscure phantoms,
    Unknown friend!
I have one friend—the road ahead of me
    In the damp fog of night.
There is no living there; as in the dark ocean there is
    Only sorrow.
I am old of soul. My long path is some sort of
    Black lot.
A heavy dream, accursed and obstinate,
    Presses on my chest.

(*6 June 1899*)

Do not shed burning tears
Over the transient grave.
The hours of visions and reveries will pass

And I will return to my darling's embrace.
Have no regrets! I am ready
To answer your passion with love
But I have found an immaculate temple
Which I will never encounter in life.
Do not call me! Worldly power
Is not capable of enchaining the poet's spirit.
I possess an unfathomable passion
Warmed by the heavens' living fire.
I will abandon you. I will soon return
To you even more blissful
And renew my love
With a vivider and more incorruptible love.
(*8 June 1899*)

 21

Why, why are the blows of fate chasing
Me into the darkness of non-being?
Can it be that all things, even my life,
Are only instants of a long punishment?
I want to live even if there is no happiness here
And nothing to gladden my heart,
But some sort of light keeps drawing me ever forward
And it is as if I can shine with it! It may be a
Phantom, but I see the yearned-for light in the distance!
All my hopes may be vain
But there—far from this world of vanity—
Its rays shine beautifully!
(*29 June 1899*)

 22

The morning wafts its breath into your little window,
My inspired heart;
Forgotten dreams fly by,

Visions of spring are resurrected,
And on a rosy cloud of reveries
Someone's soul has been carried through the heights
By a young god, recently born…
Leave your pernicious chamber,
Fly into the infinite heights,
Chase the winged vision;
The morning knows your aspiration,
My inspired heart!
(*5 August 1899*)

 23

*To K. M. S.*

Do you remember the agitated city,
The distant blue haze?
You and I were walking in silence
On that false road…
We were walking—the moon kept rising
Higher beyond the dark fence.
The road seemed false—
I did not return.
Our love was deceived
Or the road carried us away.
It is just that the city's blue murk
Has again stirred in me…
Do you remember the agitated city,
The distant blue haze?
You and I were walking imprudently
On that false road…
(*23 August 1899*)

 24

The city's asleep, shrouded in darkness;
The street lamps flicker dimly…
Over there in the distance, beyond the Neva,

[16]

I see glimmers of dawn.
In this distant reflection,
In these glimmers of fire,
Lying in wait is the awakening
Of days of anguish for me...
(*23 August 1899*)

 25

*To an Unknown God*

Are you not the one who will revive the soul?
Are you not the one who will reveal mysteries to her?
Are you not the one who will bewing the songs
That are so insane, so accidental?

Oh, believe! I will give you my life
When to this unfortunate poet
You open the door into a new temple,
Pointing out the path from darkness to light!...

Are you not the one who into a distant land,
Into a land unknown to me now,
Will lead me—I will gaze into the distances
And cry out: "It is God. The desert is at an end!"
(*22 September 1899*)

 26

The evening shadows have not yet spread
But the moon already shines on the water.
Everything is mistier and more superstitious
In the soul and in the heart—everywhere...
Superstition begets desires,
And in the misty and pure everywhere
The heart senses the bliss of the rendezvous,
The pale moon shines on the water...

Someone whispers, sings, and admires;
I hold my breath—
In this shining some great thing is sensed,
But I have already experienced a great thing…
And only now, as the evening shadows
Start to spread more boldly,
Do the inspirations of the deceived days
Arise for an instant more superstitious…
(*5 October 1899*)

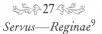
## 27
### Servus—Reginae[9]

Do not call. Even without being called
    I will go into the temple.
I will bow my head in silence
    To your feet.

I will listen to your commands
    And wait meekly.
I will grasp at our momentary meetings
    And desire again.

I am subjugated by the power of your passions,
    Beneath the yoke I am weak.
At times—your servant; at times—your beloved;
    But eternally—your slave.
(*14 October 1899*)

## 28
### To My Mother

The darkness has descended, pregnant with mists.
The winter night is dim and not foreign to my heart.

---

9 "Servant to the queen."

My orphaned spirit is seized by the uselessness of work,
By anguished repose, by some sort of loss.

How will you discover what ails my soul
And, dear friend, how will you heal its wounds?
Neither you nor I, through the winter mists,
Can see why my anguish is so strong.

And are our minds capable of believing that a scourge
Has been imposed on us for someone's sin?
That repose itself is anguished, and we are pressed down to the earth
By useless work and unfathomable loss?
(*22 November 1899*)

 29

For now, with tranquil step
I walk and think and sing,
Laugh at the pitiful crowd
And do not give it my sighs.

For now, my soul is still warm
And destiny commands me to protect in myself
My imperishable poetic gift
And the grandiloquent speeches of the stage…[10]
(*28 November 1899*)

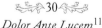 30

*Dolor Ante Lucem*[11]

Every evening, as soon as sunset fades,
I say farewell, burning with the desire for death,

10  At this time Blok was a budding actor, putting on domestic productions of
Shakespeare and other famous playwrights.
11  "Anguish before the dawn."

And again, at the dawn of the cold day,
Life will seize me and torture me!

I say farewell to what is good and to what is evil,
Feeling the hope and the terror of separation from the earthly,
But in the morning I will meet the earth again
In order to curse evil and yearn in anguish for the good!...

O God, full of power and might,
Have you really ordered the lives of all of us in such a way
That mortals, full of morning reveries,
Yearn in anguish for you without repose?...
(*3 December 1899*)

 31

The autumnal day descends in leisurely sequence,
The yellow leaves swirl down in a leisurely way,
The day is transparently fresh and the air is wondrously pure—
My soul will not escape the invisible decay.

Thus, every day my soul grows older
And every year, as the yellow leaves swirl down,
I imagine and recall and think
That the autumns of former years were not this sad.
(*5 January 1900*)

 32

Summer afternoons I gaze with fascination
At the bright sun and the blue distances,
And those sunny distances rend my soul
With an incomprehensible sorrow...

Who can understand and measure with his eye
What lies beyond those blue distances?

A dream of the far away
With an incomprehensible sorrow...
( *17 February 1900* )

 33

This day of strict precision you go out
To look at pensive nature.
On your features lies the shadow
Of forest captivity and freedom.

Your day is clear and great
And illumined by some sort of light,
But at every instant in this light
Visions come—without response.

No one will touch your repose
And disturb the strict shadow.
And you will merge with a star
On the way to the place of visions.
( *25 February 1900* )

 34

Clouds sail lazily and heavily
In the blue heat of the heavens.
My road is arduous and long,
The forest is in motionless anguish.

My horse is tired and snorts under me—
When will I arrive at my cozy home?
And over there, far away, where the forest is thick,
Someone is singing a song.

And it seems that if the voice were to grow silent,
I wouldn't be able to breathe

And my horse, snorting, would fall on the road
And I would never get home!

Clouds sail lazily and heavily
And all around me is the anguished forest.
My road is arduous and long
But the song is my companion and friend.
(*27 February 1900*)

 35

We were walking on the azure road,
Except that we parted long ago…
Into the pitch-black stormy night
A window suddenly opened…
Is that you, indistinct vision?
My heart has barely had time to cool…
I feel the passionate breathing,
I hear the old words…
The wind carries the moans away,
Mixing tears with rain…
Shall we embrace in farewell?
Shall we recall the past together?
Go away, azure vision!
The heart is constricted by anguish
On this pitch-black stormy night
By the wind and by the former image!
(*28 February 1900*)

 36

The morning eye has opened
And light pours without end.
My spirit flies there, to the East,
To meet the creator's thoughts.
When I greet the day with prayer

In the luminous morning,
I will go in spiritual purity
To meet the new-born.
And after the earthly pilgrimage
In rays of evening fire,
It is easy for the soul to return
To the prayer of yesterday.
(*14 March 1900*)

 37

I was walking in the murk of the rainy night
And in the old house, at the window,
I recognized the pensive eyes
Of my anguish.—In tears, alone,
She was gazing into the damp distances...
I admired her without end
As if I had recognized my former youth
In the features of her face.
She looked at me. I felt a pang in my heart,
The light went out—and dawn came.
The damp morning started knocking
At her forgotten window.
(*15 March 1900*)

 38

This night two people like sorrowful shadows
Walked past on the same path
Though they were destined by fate
For opposite poles of the earth.

They parted at the hour of dawn
And each preserved in silence
A testament and ideal
Absolutely alien to the other...

Interwoven by chance in the shadows,
Like leaves with alien leaves,
They keep striving secretly in the rays of dawn
To regain their habitual appearance.
(*19 March 1900*)

 39

The poet is in exile and in doubt
At the crossing of two roads.
The nighttime impressions fade,
The dawn is pale and far away.

There is no guidance in the past
About what to desire or where to go.
And in doubt and in exile
He has stopped at the crossroads.

But in his eyes there already burns a hope
Barely accessible to the mind—
The hope that the day will awake and that he will open
His eyes and catch a glimpse of the distances.
(*31 March 1900*)

 40

Though as before the singer
Of strange far-away songs of life
Wears his lyrical wreath
In dark and obscure verses—
The poet, on the other hand, approaches his goal,
Strives toward it, drawn by truth,
And suddenly sees a new world
Beyond distances previously unfamiliar.
(*5 April 1900*)

41

The shore can barely be seen.
    Float on, my boat!
Float on without trepidation—
    My sleep is deep.
Its repose will not be disturbed
    By the mountain of waves
Crashing down with a moan
    On my poor boat.
Through the pure and deep mist
    Float on, my boat.
It is of immortality in my far-away sleep
    That I dream.
(*1 May 1900*)

 42

A midnight star rolled down the sky
Without leaving a trace...
The window opened noiselessly...
Farewell, my winged dream!
You are still here but will melt away.
To my doubts on my road,
As long as you keep breathing the night into yourself,
I will keep saying: farewell...
I will keep believing: your tender image
Will not melt away before morning comes:
Some angel is spreading
Nighttime pearls before me.
(*16 May 1900*)

 43

My soul is all illumined, as before,
By the unfading radiance of former days.

But the early fall, pensively sorrowful,
Has breathed its anguished air at me.
The break-up is near. The night is dark.
But I keep hearing in the distance, as in those young days:
"The fair Ophelia.—Nymph, in thy orisons
Be all my sins rememb'red."[12]
And my soul is filled, in agitation and in vain,
With a distant and beautiful remembrance.
(*28 May 1900*)

Do not summon or promise
Past inspiration to the soul.
I am a solitary son of earth,
You are a radiant vision.

The earth is desolate, the night is pale,
Motionless is the lunar glow,
The stars are a place of mute quietude,
A place of fear and silence.

I know your triumphant countenance,
I clearly hear your summoning voice,
My soul understands your language
But you call me in vain.

The earth is desolate, the night is pale,
Do not expect the past enchantment:
In my soul is reflected
The place of fear and silence.
(*2 June 1900*)

12 *Hamlet* 3:1. Allusion to the domestic production of *Hamlet* in which Blok played
the Dane and Liubov Dmitrievna Mendeleeva played Ophelia.

45

In the hours of the evening mist
In wind and fire
A winged angel from the Koran's pages
Flies down onto my dead soul.

My mind is filled with languid impotence,
My soul flies and flies...
Numberless wings hum all around me
And a mysterious song resounds.
(*3 June 1900*)

 46

The sky is lit up. It is the dead of night.
A mass of forest trees crowds round me
But the noise from the distant unfamiliar city
Distinctly reaches me.

You recognize the heavy row of houses,
The towers, the crenellations of the severe slaughterhouses,
The dark gardens behind the stone fences,
And the proud walls of the monumental centuries-old buildings.

It is thus that out of the depths of the centuries
The inquisitive mind distinctly prepares for rebirth
The forgotten din of cities that have perished
And the return movement of existence.
(*10 June 1900*)

 47

Do not entrust your paths
To the numberless crowd of flatterers:
They will destroy your palace
And extinguish your altar's sacred flame.

Those who are strong of spirit
Flee the rabble or light
Their fires on mountain tops,
Tearing asunder the veils of darkness.
(*25 June 1900*)

 48

I will observe the destruction
Of the universe, my homeland,
And I will rejoice in solitude
At the terrible funeral of existence.

I may be solitary but my age is joyous,
In love, as it is, with annihilation.
Indeed, I, not unlike a few great men,
Am a witness to the universe's destruction.
(*26 June 1900*)

 49

Everything has perished. The burning orb,
As before, produces the progression of the years.
At the bottom of the hill the sorrowful grave
Laments the passing of the former beautiful existence.
In the black night a white phantom awaits
Other shades in silence and in melancholy.

You will acquire, whitening shade,
Crowds of others who have lost existence.
The night will pass, the long day will awake—
Again in its burning heat the orb of day,
The fiery orb, will rise
And burn the anguished land.
(*2 July 1900*)

[28]

50

It was an echo of my young days
Awakening in my soul and then fading,
And in the shining of the morning rays
The night seemed mute.

It was the pre-morning sleep departing
And my spirit, at the boundary of awakening,
Springing up, crying out, and regaining
That vision from long ago.

It was a pitiless stream
Of immortal thoughts beyond any doubts.
And it rushed away, having awakened
Crowds of forgotten revelations.

It was infinitude carrying hurricanes
Over my fallen spirit.
It was the Eternally Young Maiden[13] passing
Into unillumined mists.
(*29 July 1900*)

51

The sunset's last purple was burning down,
The last wind sighed deeply,
The clouds opened up, the moon rose,
A song was being sung in the distance.

All the hopes of my young years
Were reborn more vivid and miraculous
But, in response, my song-tormented soul
Was filled with sorrow.
In the distance there was a flash of light from the old god

13  One of the names of the Eternal Feminine to which the young Blok was devoted.

And above the sinister lightning
A siege of plangently weeping cranes
Was flying south.
(*4 August 1900*)

**52**

Not satiated with streams of blood,
The land is silent.
I walk ahead with hurried step,
I seek fields free of victims.

But like a prisoner confined in a dungeon
I seek in vain: there is nothing but blood and darkness!
Only the bloody dawn presents a sign—
Mysterious and obscure.
(*14 August 1900*)

**53**
*Agrapha Dogmata*[14]

I've seen the dark of day and the light of night.
I've seen the horror of eternal doubt,
As well as the Lord with soul torn to pieces
In the smoke of disbelief and confusion.

It was the dawn of a great birth
When the unnumbered chaos of the worlds
Vanished in an infinitude of torment
And all things mysteriously grumbled and rushed ahead.

A heavy flame enveloped the universe
And thunder stopped the rushing creations.
A mute boundary was installed to the end.
Out of the dark came the sage's mind

---

14 "Unwritten dogmas."

And on the mountain peaks—without fear or exertion—
The wings of glistening ideas fluttered for him.
(*22 August 1900*)

Your image appears spontaneously
Amid the familiar banal days.
Sometimes it's easy, sometimes painful,
Not to bow down to the ground before You.

In my forgetfulness without sadness
I cannot forget sometimes
How inconsolably my constellations
Sorrowed over You.

You lived not in my agitation
But in that land native to us—
And in solitary veneration
I came to know Your truth.
(*22 September 1900*)

The night shook with the storm and fires of lightning
Illumined the row of distant hills;
Only in the morning did I lift the lifeless corpse
And bury it at the foot of the hills, at the edge of the land.

The day passed silent and mysteriously fresh.
The evening brought a pitch-black darkness,
And at the edge of the land, above the hills in the distance,
I heard the lifeless voice of anguish.

I tried to break through the enchanted circle
And cross over the boundary of the total darkness

But in the morning all breath went out of me in the distance
As I lay stretched out in agitation at the edge of the land.
(*24 September 1900*)

 56

Smoke rises from the altars and incense from the censers
    Of the children of earth.
The goddess of life, the mysterious heavenly body,
    Is in the distance.
They sing solemnly and triumphantly glorify
    The mute firmament.
They grasp at the desolate air with their hands,
    Receiving death.
Ungraspable, she is not among us;
    She is beyond the earth,
While we, calling with triumphant words,
    Lie in dust.
(*29 September 1900*)

 57

You were at the window,
    Pure and tender,
Reigning over the noisy crowd.
    I stood forgotten
    And hidden by the crowd
In a veneration of love before you.

    It seemed to me then
    That now and always
You gazed in front of you without a thought in your head,
    While below, at the window,
    The people swayed before you
Like a wave of the sea.

Made proud by the veneration,
    You always seemed
A solitary and powerful dream.
    And no one heard
    The sound of your voice—
You dominated the crowd in silence.

    I stood forgotten
    And hidden by the crowd.
You gazed in front of you without a thought in your head,
    Pure and tender,
    While below, at the window,
People stood agitated around me.
(*12 October 1900*)

 58

Though I was an admirer of the Greeks, I'd forget my lyre
When you'd block my path with a word.
I'd sigh before you about happiness
And you'd be contemptuously silent.

A fire burned in my soul but you were dark.
And I, suffering meekly,
Thought: at some point like a tuned string you'd
Respond agreeably to my call.

But you passed by me in silence
And, as then, with a single reminder
You tear to pieces now and sometimes torture
My Greek confessions.
(*12 October 1900*)

59

I know, death is near. And you
Will not have contempt for me now.
You will condescend from your purity
To my anguished end.

But your love is dark for me,
Your confessions are unusual.
Can you find in your heart names
For uncustomary words and caresses?

What if you find the words
And I, slightly dying,
Start appealing, in an act of late tenderness,
For a new resurrection?
(*15 October 1900*)

 60

It is time to return to the former battle:
Let the spirit rise and the flesh sleep!
Let us replace all these happy days
With constant prayer!

But let us preserve deep in the soul
All these joyful days:
The caresses of the black-eyed girl
And the bright lights illuminating the stage!
(*22 October 1900*)

 61

Renounce your favorite creations,
Renounce people and social encounters.
Renounce worldly desires.
Think in the daytime and pray at night.

If your spirit is filled with troubled ardor,
Chase inspiration away.
Only wisdom is worthy of
Passing into inevitable night.

On earth you will not know reward.
With spirit clear before the face of God,
Keep burning to the end, abandoning the icon lamp,
With a solitary and true fire.
(*1 November 1900*)

62

Worn down by the storm of inspiration,
Burned by earthly fire,
With a cold thirst for redemption
I knocked at the Lord's door.
The pagan had become a Christian
And, wounded, he hastened
To cast to the ground before the One
The remainder of his enfeebled powers.
I knock at the threshold of the ideal,
There is no answer... but there, in the distance,
The veil of the barely abandoned earth
Beckons and glimmers...
The Lord did not hear my prayer
But I feel that the powers of the passionate days
Have breathed into the face of one wounded in battle
And have again spread throughout my soul.
I do not understand the joy of paradise,
The future darkness, the peace of the grave...
Back! A young pagan beauty
Is calling me to a friendly feast!
(*3 November 1900*)

63

In those chaste years
I came to understand the mysterious meaning of life,
Your admirer, like you a child of freedom,
Distant from strict numbers.

Or have those years passed
So that, having fallen out of love with freedom,
I gaze into future sorrows
And am numbering, numbering without you?

So be it! Let the past be forgotten—
The meaning of life is not in the present!
I will not attain reconciliation,
You will not understand the accursed numbers!
(*15 November 1900*)

64

My monastery, where I languish godlessly,
Is granite melted under the extreme heat of reason.
I am suffocating. It is dark for me under this false heat.
I am leaving for another burning skete...[15]

There will be heat there, but it will be the usual heat of earth.
The bloody sphere will melt my brain to the end
And I will lose my mind more calmly and fearlessly
Than here, where flesh and blood have failed.
Where is the new skete? Where is my new monastery?
Not in the heavens, where there is only the darkness of the grave,
But on earth; it is vulgar and healthy,
And I will find everything there when I lose my mind!
(*17 November 1900*)

---

15 A skete is a monastic community that allows relative isolation for monks, but also allows for communal services and the safety of shared resources and protection.

### ❦ 65 ❦

#### *To O. M. Solovyova*[16]

I seek salvation.
My fires burn on the mountain peaks—
They illuminate the whole realm of night.
But brighter than all is the spiritual gaze in me
And You[17] are in the distance. But is it You?
      I seek salvation.

The stellar choir resounds joyously in heaven.
I am cursed by human generations.
I have lit a bonfire for You in the mountains,
      But You are a vision.
      I seek salvation.

I am tired of resounding, the stellar choir grows silent.
The night passes. Doubt flees.
There You descend from the distant luminous mountains.
I have awaited You. I have stretched out my spirit to You.
      In You is salvation!
( *25 November 1900* )

### ❦ 66 ❦

Slowly, heavily, and faithfully
Departing into the black night,
Filled with immeasurable hope,
Repeating the words of a prayer,
I know that prayer will
Always help lucid hope
And that heavy faithfulness will ground
The slow stone of toil.

---

16  The wife of M.S. Solovyov, a brother of the great philosopher Vladimir Solovyov.
At this time Blok was very close to the family of M.S. Solovyov.

17  The Eternal Feminine, or Sophia.

Slowly, heavily, and faithfully
I measure the nocturnal paths:
One filled with immeasurable faith
Can reach his destination by morning.
(*5 December 1900*)

Tomorrow with the first ray
Of the sun rising in the sky
   There will rise in my heart
   An immense power.
My spirit will shake the ether
And the universe's mute forgetfulness;
   Approaching is the world
   Of my renewal.
   I will light the censer
   And strap on a sword
Tomorrow with the first ray
Of the sun rising in the sky.
(*6 December 1900*)

Begotten in the dead of night
By the earth's pale satellite,
Clothed in the fabric of earth,
You gleamed like silver in the distance.

I was walking toward the leafless north,
I was walking in frosty dust.
 I heard your mysterious voice,
You gleamed like silver in the distance.

Begotten in the dead of night,
You gleamed like silver in the distance.

Your tortured soul became
The fabric of frosty earth.

Greeks, sleepless gods,
Rise in the frosty dust!
Drunk with your sun,
Pour the sun out in the distance!

Greeks, sleepy Greeks,
Pour the sun out in the distance!
The defeated soul has become
A clod of the cold earth!
(*24 December 1900*)

### *To K. M. S.*

You will not deceive, pale phantom,
Well tested passions.
Your disordered appearance, poor image,
Will not astonish my soul.
I know the distant past
But I do not expect explosions of passion
In the near future. That which is young
Has passed, and in your tired and unnecessary
But beckoning phantom I cannot find fire.
You can torture me only
As an oppressive conceit.
(*25 December 1900*)

You too, my young one, my sad one,
    Are departing!
Greetings to you, greetings of farewell,
    I send this night.

And I am that very same weary guest
    Of the strange earth.
I wander, like a tardy pilgrim,
    After beauty.
She glitters and laughs
    But I have only one care:
That my wine not spill out of
    My cup.
Meanwhile there is silence all around,
    My cup is empty,
And death's early summons
    Is repeated by the lips.
You too, my young one, my sad one,
    Are departing.
And I, an accidental guest, depart after you
    As before—into the night.
(*31 December 1900*)

# Verses about the Beautiful Lady
## (1901–1902)

*Introduction*

Rest is impossible. The road is steep.
The evening is beautiful. I knock at the gate.

A stranger to earthly knocking and stern,
You are scattering pearls all around.

The tower is high and the sunset is frozen in time.
A red mystery lies at the entrance.

Who at sunset set afire this tower
That was erected by the Empress Herself?

Every little figure on the decorative carving
Throws a red flame toward you.

The cupola soars into the azure heights.
The blue windows are afire with a blush.

All the bells are clanging.
Her sunset-less attire is flooded with spring.

Was it you who waited for me at the sunsets?
Set afire the tower? Opened the gate?
(*28 December 1903*)

# I

PETERSBURG, SPRING 1901

 1

I went out. Winter twilight
Was slowly descending on the earth.
Young happenings of former days
Came trustingly out of the darkness...

They came and stood behind my shoulders
And sang with the wind about the spring...
I walked with soft steps,
Glimpsing eternity in the depths...

O living happenings of my best days!
To your song out of the depths
Twilight descended onto the earth
And dreams of eternity rose!
(*25 January 1901, Petersburg*)

 2

The wind brought from afar
A hint of springtime song.
Somewhere a patch of sky
Opened brightly and deep.

In this bottomless azure,
In the twilight of approaching spring,
Winter storms were weeping,
Stellar dreams were hovering.

Timidly, darkly, and deeply
My strings were weeping.
The wind brought from afar
Your sonorous songs.
(*29 January 1901*)

[42]

Evening shadows spread gently
Over blue snows.
Crowds of disordered visions
Have disturbed your ashes.
You are sleeping beyond the distant plain,
You are sleeping in linens of snow…
I imagine I hear the sounds
Of your swan song.
A voice calling in agitation,
An echo in the cold snows.
Is it possible to rise from the dead?
Is the past not ashes?
No, out of the Lord's house
The dear and familiar spirit,
Full of immortality, came out
To agitate my hearing with its song.
Crowds of visions of the grave,
Sounds of living voices…
Evening shadows touch gently
The blue snows.
(*2 February 1901*)

My soul is silent. In the cold sky
The same stars burn for it.
All around the noisy nations shout
About gold or bread…
My soul is silent—it listens to the shouts
And gazes at the distant worlds,
But in two-faced solitude
It is preparing wondrous gifts,
Gifts for its gods,
And silent and in tranquility
It catches with its tireless hearing
The distant call of another soul…

[ 43 ]

In the same way the inseparable hearts
Of white birds over the ocean
Exchange a call beyond the mist
Which only they can fully understand.
(*3 February 1901*)

 5

Now, filled with bliss,
Before the divine palace
I await the beautiful angel
With his sword of glad tidings.

Now, show mercy, O God,
To your blessed slave!
Angels have come out, O God,
With gently white wings!

God! God!
Believe my prayer,
My soul burns in it!
Free from his pitiful battle
Your weary slave!
(*15 February 1901*)

 6

I have understood your aspirations—
I am standing in your way.
A fire of unearthly desires
Makes your maidenly breast tremble.
What chance do my weak and pitiful words have
In their battle with your flame
On the threshold of any unpredictable meeting
With a dear and alien principle?
I have understood everything, and withdraw.

Blessed is the day to come.
Rejoicing in red twilight,
You have missed the shadows of night.
But the maidenly vestment is visible,
My day with you is spent...
My soul may be unhealable—
But blessed is this dream which is over.
(*26 February 1901*)

You are withdrawing into the red twilight,
Into infinite circles.
I hear the light echo,
The far-away footsteps.

Are you lost near or far
Away in the heights?
Should one expect, or not, a sudden meeting
In this sonorous silence?

In the silence the far-away footsteps
Grow louder.
Is it you closing, aflame,
The infinite circles?
(*6 March 1901*)

My prophecy has come to pass:
Before the future grave
Your sanctuary has been lighted
One more time by a mysterious power.

I am filled with exultation,
I am drunk with the great mystery

And know firmly that my prophetic words
Have come to pass—not by chance.
(*7 March 1901*)

### *To My Mother*

The more my rebellious soul ails,
    The clearer the worlds.
The azure god, pure and gentle,
    Sends his gifts.

Filled with gentleness,
    He sends woes and sorrows.
But through them one's gaze can see
    Into other distances.

And the agitated soul ails more,
    But clearer are the worlds.
This is the gentle azure God
    Sending his gifts.
(*8 March 1901*)

### 10

It was not for nothing that I was afraid to open
The window into the inclement midnight.
As in the old days, I had to poison
What was full of hope.

I will be tormented by the former thought
In the inclement midnight darkness,
But I will burn with a world of prayer
And hide on this earth.

In my unceasing prayer
Under your hostile power,
I will hide the repository of my thoughts
From men and from beasts.
(*1 April 1901*)

 11

*To O. M. Solovyova*

On a dark and wild night,
A son of bottomless depth,
A pale-faced phantom roams about
The fields of my land,
And the fields in the great murk
Are strange, cold, and dark.

But sometimes, hearing God,
A daughter of the blessed land
From her native palace
Chases away the phantom dreams,
And in the fields shimmer many
Pure maidens of spring.
(*23 April 1901*)

 12

On a cold day, an autumn day,
I will return there
To remember that springtime sigh,
To see the former image.

I will come, and will not weep.
Remembering, I will not be consumed by fire.
With a random song I will greet
The dawn of the new autumn.

Time's evil laws
Have lulled to sleep my sorrowful spirit.
The former wails, the old moans,
Can no longer be heard—I am extinguished.

Fire itself will not burn my blind
Eyes with the former dream.
Day is darker than night
For one whose soul is asleep.
(*27 April 1901, the field beyond Staraia Derevnia*)

### 13

*So they parted at the hour of dawn.*
(A.B.)[1]

Earthly dreams keep flying away,
Strange lands keep getting closer,
Cold mute lands
Without love and without spring.

There—far away, having opened their eyes,
Visions of near and dear ones
Pass into new dungeons
And look around indifferently.

There a mother does not recognize her son,
Passionate hearts will be extinguished;
There will cease without hope
My wandering without end...

And suddenly at the threshold of the prison
I will hear far-away steps...
You—solitary—in the distance
Will close the last circles...
(*4 May 1901*)

1 The epigraph belongs to Blok himself.

### 14

All being and that which is[2] are in harmony
In a great unceasing silence.
Gaze there with interest or with indifference,
It's all the same to me—the universe is within me.
I feel and believe and know that
You cannot tempt a seer with sympathy.
I myself unconditionally contain within myself
All the fires with which you burn.
But there is no longer any weakness or any strength;
The past and the future are within me.
All being and that which is are frozen
In a great unchanging silence.
And here at the end, full of a seer's sight,
I crossed the boundary.
I am only awaiting the guiding vision
To fly away into another void.
(*17 May 1901*)

### 15

Someone is whispering and laughing
Through the azure mist.
Whenever I grow sad in my quietude—
Again laughter comes to me from dear places!

Again whispering—and in the whispers
There is someone's caress, as in a dream;
In someone's feminine breathing.
Clearly, joy is to be mine forever!

Whisper and laugh a little, dear,
Dear image, tender dream;

---

2 "Being" (bytie) and "that which is" (sushchee) are terms borrowed from the philo-
sophical writings of Vladimir Solovyov.

With an unearthly power, clearly,
You are endowed and bewinged.
(*20 May 1901*)

 16

This white night a red moon
Floats out into the blueness.
Transparently beautiful, it wanders
And is reflected in the Neva.

I foresee and dream about
The fulfillment of mysterious thoughts.
Do you bring something good,
O red moon, quiet noise?
(*22 May 1901*)

# II

The heavenly is not measurable by the mind,
The azure is hidden from minds.
Only rarely do seraphim bring
Holy dreams to the chosen of the worlds.

And I imagined the Russian Venus,
Entwined in a heavy tunic,
Passionless in her purity, joyless without measure,
The features of her face expressing a tranquil dream.

She has come down to earth not for the first time
But crowding round her for the first time
Are her new heroes and champions...
And strange is the gleam of her deep eyes...
(*29 May 1901, Shakhmatovo*)

They make noise, they celebrate,
Never growing tired;
They exult in victory,
They are forever blissful.
Who can discover in the surrounding din,
Who can sense if only for a brief instant
My harmonious language,
Infinite in its mysterious womb?
Let my freedom be strange to everyone,
Let myself be strange to everyone in my garden—
But nature's clamor is uproarious
And I am her coparticipant in everything!
(*30 May 1901*)

### 19

Lonely, I come to you,
Bewitched by the fires of love.
You are divining. Do not summon me.
I myself have long been telling my own fortune.

From the heavy burden of the years
It is fortune-telling alone that has saved me.
And again I am telling my fortune with regard to you,
But the answer is unclear and obscure.

I cherish the days and years in thrall
To divining—do not summon me...
But will the fires of dark bewitched
Love soon be extinguished?
(*1 June 1901, Shakhmatovo*)

### 20

*Yearning and loving, you will shake off*
*The heavy dream of everyday-life consciousness.*
Vladimir Solovyov[3]

I have a presentiment of You. The years are passing by
But I have a presentiment of You in the same single image.

The whole horizon is on fire—and unbearably clear;
And I wait silently—"yearning and loving."

The whole horizon is on fire, and Your coming is at hand,
But I am terrified that You will change Your image,

That You will provoke an impudent suspicion
By altering, in the end, Your usual features.
Oh, what if I fall—sorrowfully and low—
Without overcoming the deathly dreams!

3 From Solovyov's poem "Why are words needed? In the azure boundlessness..."

How clear the horizon is! The radiance is at hand.
But I am terrified that You will change Your image.
(*4 June 1901, Shakhmatovo*)

 21

It is late and dark. I will abandon without desires
God's house which is uproarious with merriment.
I will get to the end of the radiant road, I will not expect encounters;
I will get there the same as I journeyed—unknown.

The last sigh, mysterious and bottomless;
The last words, the last clear gaze—
And darkness all around, illumined by dream,
And the radiant years will never be retrieved.

Yet into another darkness, this time without the former strength,
I go away wordlessly, having abandoned the clear shore,
And it will not be visible, perhaps, until the grave
Or perhaps it will never be encountered again.
(*6 June 1901*)

 22

And I, unfaithful, yearned and sorrowed
And, filled with the poetic impulse,
Abandoned without need
My native haunts.

But my heart sensed a language that
My ears could not hear—in solitude;

And in belated tenderness
I returned—and understood.
(*9 June 1901*)

### 23

*...it is too late to desire:*
*Everything has passed, both joy and grief.*
Vladimir Solovyov[4]

Do not be angry and forgive. You blossom in solitude
   And I too will never retrieve
Those golden dreams, that profound faith…
   Hopeless is my path.

Blossoming with your sleepy thought, your bliss is great,
   You are strong with azure.
For me there are another life and another road,
And my soul has no taste for sleep.

Believe: there are no young worshippings more unhappy than mine
   In this large land,
Where your mysterious genius, indifferent to me,
   Breathed and loved.
(*10 June 1901*)

### 24

Say your prayer full of mystery—
The rays of your last dawn
Are already near.
Prepare yourself, think, and be silent.
Prepared, thoughtful, and mute,
Look upward for the last time;
God does not want you to be extinguished
Without meeting here your former Love.
As in the first time, so for the last
You will enter Her chamber
And come to know—as is God's desire—
Her extraordinary eyes.
(*10 June 1901*)

4  From Solovyov's poem "On the Deck of the Fritiofa."

25

Beyond the mist, beyond the woods,
A light flashes at times—and vanishes again.
I am riding through damp fields—
And there it flashes again from afar.

Like lights wandering
Late at night beyond the river
Above the sorrowing meadows,
I and You have our rendezvous.

But even at night there is no response;
You'll disappear in the river reeds,
Carrying away the source of light;
And then you'll beckon to me from afar again.
(*14 June 1901*)

 26

In its inertia of youth, in its pre-dawn laziness,
The soul soared upward and found the Star there.
The evening was misty; shadows were spreading softly;
The Evening Star, silent, waited.

Imperturbable, You went out onto the dark
Steps and, Quiet One, floated up.
And by a wavering reverie in the pre-dawn laziness
You rose to the stellar paths.

And the night flowed on in a mist of dreams.
And timid youth had no end of reveries.
And dawn was approaching. And the shadows were fleeing.
And, Clear One, You flowed with the sun.
(*19 June 1901*)

What god do you serve?
Is it the pre-dawn excitement
And the pre-sunset reveries
That you find dear in your soaring?
Or, merging with a star,
Are you a goddess, priding yourself
On a beauty equal to that of the gods
And gazing with indifferent eyes
From unearthly heights
Upon the flaming shadows
Of earthly prayers and worship
Addressed to you, O empress of purity?
(*20 June 1901*)

Today You were walking alone
And I did not see Your wonders.
Above Your high hill
Stretched jagged woods.

That forest, dense with trees,
And those mountain trails
Prevented me from merging with the unknown
And from blossoming with your azure.
(*22 June 1901*)

*To S. Solovyov*[5]

She grew beyond the distant mountains.
The wild valley was her native land.
None of you with your burning eyes

5  Sergei Mikhailoviich Solovyov (1885–1941), a cousin of Blok and a nephew of
Vladimir Solovyov. At this time he was a close friend of Blok.

Saw her—she grew alone.
And only the face of the immortal sun
Gazed each day at her maidenly blooming;
A moist plant, she ascended toward the sun
And had a secret trace of it in herself.
And she departed into death, desiring and sorrowing.
None of you saw her earthly ashes...
Suddenly she blossomed, exulting in the azure,
In other distances and on unearthly mountains.
And now she is all dusted with snow.
Who, O madmen, has visited the white temple?
She blossomed beyond the distant mountains,
She flows amid the other stars.
(*26 June 1901*)

 30

I remember that sleepless hour of night;
Years have passed but the memory of it is still fresh.
Darkness reigned but my eyes wouldn't close.
My mind was racing and my heart couldn't care less about sleep.

Suddenly from afar, out of the silence of future half-dreams,
There drifted into my cell
An indistinct sound of incoherent praying,
An unfamiliar wingless terrifying call.

Was it the moan of a godlessly savage soul
And did our hearts not already meet then?
I know you, my two-faced confidant,
My dear friend, hostile to the end.
(*27 June 1901, Boblovo*)

31

You were summoned to strange lands
And set off on the long journey.
We saw you off hopelessly
And many were sighing.

Winter stole up on us imperceptibly
And with the first snow from the yard
You took away all the sacred ardor
By which we were living yesterday.

Farewell, we are looking at the road
But the blizzard is wiping out all tracks.
We will return little by little
To the godless laziness of past years,

And we will no longer practice magic
Over the mystical enigma
Or, late at night, having gotten up on the sly,
Dream in the light of the pale moon.
(*28 June 1901*)

32

Listening to the call of the confused life
Secretly swirling within me,
I will not give myself to any false and momentary
Thought even in my dreams.
I await the wave that will carry me
Down into the radiant depths.

Knees bent, gaze meek,
 Heart quiet, I keep track only slightly
Of the receding shadows
Of the world's vain affairs
Amid the visions, dreams,
And voices of other worlds.
(*3 July 1901*)

33

Transparent unfamiliar shadows
Float toward You and You float with them
Into the embrace of azure dreams
Incomprehensible to us—You are giving Yourself.

Before You is the endless blue
Of seas, fields, mountains, and woods;
Birds call to one another in the unbounded heights;
The mist rises, the heavens redden.

And here below, in the dust, in the nothingness,
Having glimpsed for an instant Your immortal features,
A negligible slave, full of inspiration,
I sing You. You do not know him,

You would not pick him out of the crowd,
You would not reward him with your smile
When, enslaved, he follows you with his eyes,
Having tasted for an instant Your immortality.
(*3 July 1901*)

 34

I await the summons, seek the answer;
The sky grows mute, the earth is silent;
Beyond the yellow field, far away somewhere,
My call awoke for an instant.

From echoes of distant words
From the nighttime sky, from slumbering fields,
I keep imagining the mysteries of the future meeting,
Of encounters clear but momentary.

I wait—and a new trembling seizes me;
The sky is brighter, the silence is deeper...

The nighttime mystery will be shattered by a word...
Have mercy, O God, on our nighttime souls!

My call awoke for an instant
Like a distant echo somewhere beyond the field.
I keep awaiting the summons, seeking the answer,
But the earth's silence lingers strangely...
(*7 July 1901*)

 35

Were you not the one, my singer, who passed in my dreams
Over the shore of the Neva and beyond the border of the capital?
Were you not the one who took away my heart's secret terror
With a warrior's courage and a maiden's gentleness?

With your endless song you melted the snows
And harmoniously repeated the early spring.
You passed by like a star to me, but one that shone in daytime rays
And sanctified the stones of the squares and streets.

I sing you, oh yes! But your light shined forth
And suddenly disappeared—into the distant mists.
I direct my gaze toward mysterious lands—

I do not see you, and there has long been no God.
But I believe you will rise and the red dusk will explode with light,
Closing the mysterious circle, belated in its movement.
(*8 July 1901*)

 36

Beyond the city in the fields the air has the breath of spring.
I walk and tremble in anticipation of fire.
There, ahead of me, I know—the breath of twilight
Agitates the sea and torments me.

I remember: in the distance is the great noise of the capital.
There, in the twilight of spring, is restless heat.
Oh, what meager hearts! What hopeless faces!
Those who have not known spring are anguishing over themselves.

But here, as a memory of great and innocent years,
Out of the twilight unknown faces
Are portending harmony of life and fires of eternity...

Let us forget the earthly noise. Come to me without wrath,
Mysterious Sunset Maiden,
And we will unite tomorrow and yesterday with fire.
(*12 July 1901*)

### 37
### *To S. Solovyov*

All may enter. In the inner chambers
There is no testament, though mystery is present.
You are dismayed by the benumbed look
Of the ancient books on the old lecterns.

In them lives the sacred mystery of God
And these ancient things will never grow corrupted.
You who are proud that you have created so much,
Your inspirer and architect is the earthly world.

It is in vain that noisy blasphemies against the creator
Have godlessly erupted out of you.
All of you, slaves of impossible freedom,
Will be dismayed here by this mystery without end.
(*14 July 1901*)

38

You passed by on sky-blue paths,
Behind you the mist is billowing.
The evening twilight above us
Has turned into the desired deception.
Above your sky-blue road
Stretches a sinister darkness.
But with deep faith in God
Even a dark church is full of light for me.
(*16 July 1901*)

 39

Do not wait for a final answer,
It does not exist in this life.
But the poet's hearing senses clearly
A distant noise on his path.

He bends his ear attentively,
Listens greedily, waits sensitively,
And it has already reached his hearing:
It blossoms, is blissful, grows...

It is coming ever closer, the expectation is growing stronger,
But, ah!—the agitation is unbearable...
And the poet falls, becoming mute,
Hearing that the noise is now close to him on his path.

Nearby is a family in fervent prayer,
And above the cemetery there is a harmonious ringing...
They will not understand the dreams
He did not wait long enough to have!
(*19 July 1901*)

40

Do not sing to me sweetly and tenderly:
It is long since I have lost all connection with this earthly vale.
The soul's seas are vast and shoreless;
Song will vanish in this shorelessness.

Only words without songs are clear to the heart.
You will blossom above the heart only with their truth.
Song's sound, importunate and passionate,
Conceals an unseen lie.

My young ardor, which you mocked,
I have abandoned—the mists are behind me.
Embrace the dreams that envelop me;
Come to understand what lies ahead.
(*25 July 1901*)

41

I regret the passing neither of joyous nor of sultry days,
Neither of mature summer nor of young spring.
They have passed—luminously and restlessly;
And they will come again—they are given by the earth.

I do regret that the great day will soon pass,
That the child scarcely born will die.
Oh, I do regret, my friend, that the future ardor will cool,
Vanishing into past darkness and into coldness.

No, I expect that at the end of my agitated wandering
I will find my path and not sigh over the day!
The sacred meeting will not be darkened
By the one who sighs over me here.
(*27 July 1901*)

42

The sign of a true miracle
At the hour of midnight darkness—
Obscure murk and a pile of stones
And you shining in them like a diamond.

And you yourself beyond the river darkness
Are directing the mountain race,
You, who shine forever
With golden azure!
(*29 July 1901, Factory*)

43

You are distant, as before, so now too.
I cannot find my native shores.
My sorrow is alien to your holy essence
And joy is not what gives a soul its value.

Severe coldness is your holy power:
Godless heat does not befit holy places.
Let love's lot be oblivion and the grave;
Above the grave you are a radiant temple.
(*11 August 1901, Dedovo*)

44

I am standing on the royal road.
It is dead of night, little lights all around me—
They are dim but I have to
Find everything by morning.

I step forward—total murk.
I step back—completely dark.

But in the distance there is a line of brightness,
And above this line is the sign that guides me.

But the path is arduous—water roars,
The woods grow black, the fields are silent…
The unattainable star—
That is the promised land…

This star is the sign that guides me,
But the lights around me are dim;
Beyond the line of brightness are other days
And I have to find everything by morning, by morning!
(*15 August 1901*)

 45

*Will the evening never come*
*With its desires and its row boats,*
*With its oars and light beyond the river?*
Fet[6]

  Dusk, springtime dusk.
  Cold waves at my feet
  And unearthly hopes in my heart.
  The waves run up on the sand.

  Sounds of a far-away song
  But I cannot distinguish what it is.
  A solitary soul is weeping
  There, on the other shore.

  Is my mystery being fulfilled,
  Is it you calling from afar?
  The row boat sways and rocks—
  Something is running on the river.

6  From Afanasy Fet's poem "In the distance there is a light beyond the river…"

There are unearthly hopes in my heart;
Someone is coming toward me—I run...
Lights gleaming, springtime dusk,
Shouts on the other shore.
(*16 August 1901*)

 46

You burn above the high mountain
And are inaccessible in Your tower.
I will gallop in when evening comes
And rapturously embrace my dream.

You, hearing me from afar,
Will light your bonfire in the evening.
I will start, faithful to Fate's commands,
To understand this game of fire.

And when, amid the darkness, sheaves
Of sparks start to swirl in the smoke,
I will gallop away with the circles of fire
And reach You in the tower.
(*18 August 1901*)

 47

I can see that the golden days have come.
All the trees stand as if illuminated.
At night a coolness rises from the earth;
In the morning the white church in the distance
Seems close and is clear in its outlines.

Someone keeps singing in the distance;
I don't understand who could be singing
But in the evening over there by the river,
In the reeds or in the dry sedge,
It seems a familiar song is being sung.

I don't want to know what it is,
And besides I don't believe familiar songs.
And I would never even understand the singer…
    As if one could hide from oneself
    A fatal loss!
(*24 August 1901*)

 48

Around me are a distant plain
And crowds of burnt stumps.
Below me is my native valley
And clouds are spreading over it.

Nothing beckons me to come,
As if the distances themselves are near.
Here between heaven and earth
Lives a grim anguish.

Day and night this anguish digs up
Sandy mounds in the fields.
At times it wails mournfully
And grows silent—for a time.

And all that will be and all that has been
Are nothing more that cold soulless ashes,
Like these stones above the grave
Of love lost in the fields.
(*25 August 1901. Village of Ivlevo*)

 49

I keep telling fortunes with regard to you
But, weary of all this divining,
I gaze into your eyes sometimes
And see a fatal flame.

Or has the great thing come to pass
And you are keeping the testament of the ages
And, illuminated, have shielded yourself
Against the turbulence of the tribes?

But I, submissive to you,
Will preserve, know this, the holy testament.
Do not leave me in the mist
Of your early years.

A sworn pledge lies between us
But, unmovable in my constancy,
I conceal a kindred flame
Beneath my poor appearance.
(*27 August 1901*)

 50

There is no end to the forest paths.
   My hope is to find before the star
   The barely perceptible trail...
I hear the blades of forest grass.

   Everywhere there is a clear rumor
Of those lost and near...
Words of passage
   Over the tops of the low firs...

Will I not find from the blades of grass
   The hidden trail?
   Here she is—the star is lighted!
There is no end to the forest paths.
(*2 September 1901, the church forest*)

# III

 51

Look—I am withdrawing into the shadows,
While you remain in doubt
And are afraid to encounter the day,
Not sensing the night's approach.

Do not expect inspired words—
I, delayed at the boundary,
Calmly await the final dreams
Forgotten here, in the earthly dungeon.

Can I preserve my dreams
And believe in earthly visions
When you, unique,
Do not believe in mortal songs?

But before me the darkness is swirling,
Not sensing transitory pain,
And you are cloudlessly luminous,
But only in immortality—not in this earthly vale.
(*20 September 1901*)

 52

The winter will pass—you will see
My plains and swamps
And say: "How beautiful!
What dead slumber!"

But remember, my young maiden, in the tranquility
Of my plains I preserved my thoughts in their purity

And, sick, agitated, and grim,
I waited in vain for your soul.

In this twilight I told my fortune,
Looked into the face of cold death,
And waited infinitely long,
Greedily gazing into the mists.

But you passed by—
Amid the swamps I preserved my thoughts in their purity,
And of this dead beauty
A grim trace remained in my soul.
(*21 September 1901*)

53

When I got out of bed this misty morning,
The sun hit me in the face.
Was it you, beloved maid,
Climbing up to me on the porch?

The heavy doors were flung open!
The wind blew through the window!
We haven't heard such joyous
Songs for too long!

With them this misty morning
The sun and the wind hit me in the face!
With them it was my beloved maid
Climbing up to me on the porch!
(*3 October 1901*)

54

The hour is early. On my path,
Unseen, a dream flares up.
I hear the beating of a seraph's wings;
The heights are transparent, the distances are clear.

From the azure palace
It is time secretly to descend.
God's white, white angel
Is sowing roses on the path.

I wait in fascinated agitation—
The mystery of the weeping woman
Will open the golden links
And reveal the wings' whiteness.
(*4 October 1901*)

 55

You are departing the earthly vale
And being offered the love of a better heart.
Do not await terrifying dreams from your new freedom—
Choirs of angels, not mortals, will come down,

Will come down and remove your hair-shirt,
A symbol of excessive earthly woes.
I, in anguish, will lose sight at the boundary
Of your unearthly, your heavenly track.

Leave behind the universe's impotence,
Your repose is now inviolable.
Before me is the limit of God-knowledge,
Inevitable dusk, black smoke.
(*6 October 1901*)

 56

The evening shadows are near again,
The clear day is burning out in the distance.
Again swarms of unearthly visions
Stir into being and fly toward me—here they are.

[71]

Why is it that before our great rendezvous
You do not open up your depths?
Or do you sense another forerunner
Of the near and certain spring?

As soon as I see the lamp in the darkness,
I will rise and, not looking, fly.
Even in the twilight, my darling, you are near
To the immutable key of life.
(*14 October 1901*)

 57

I stole the burden like a thief in the night,
And I smashed unhappiness to pieces,
But—God!—how hard it is to pay attention to
Another's growing passion!

The wave, coming in, breaks
Mercilessly at my feet
And greedily sprays me,
Powerless one, with its cold foam.

I do not know if azure happiness
Lives beyond that distant boundary...
Now I am paying attention
To another's ever-growing passion.
(*14 October 1901*)

 58

I[7] preserved amid the young harmonies
The pensive and gentle form of the day.
The wind gusted, dust started flying,
And there is no sun and it is dark all around me.

7  The subject is feminine.

But in my cell it is May and I live unseen,
Alone, in flowers and await another spring.
Go away—I sense the presence of a seraph;
Alien to me here are your earthly dreams.

Go away, wanderers, children, gods!
I will blossom again on the last day,
My dreams are holy palaces,
My love is a shadow growing mute.
(*17 October 1901*)

 59

Slowly through the church doors
I[8] walked, unfree in soul;
Love songs were being sung,
Crowds of common folk were praying.

Or was it that at the moment of unbelief
He eased my burden?
Now I often go through
The church doors without doubt.

The evening roses fall,
They fall gently, slowly.
As for me, I pray more superstitiously,
I weep and repent in agony.
(*17 October 1901*)

 60

I catch the fine dust of hope,
You walk less rapidly,
But through eyes closed shut
The words burn: "Not a friend, but an enemy."

8  The subject is feminine.

When the burning stops, the truth is closer.
Or forgettable dreams
Pass slowly—and my burning is lower
While yours is higher.

Then, in salvific forgetting,
A smile roams about the face.
For tomorrow a new torment:
A yearning for the wedding crown.
(*2 November 1901*)

 61

The door creaked. My hand trembled.
I[9] went out into the sleepy streets.
Up there in the heavens clouds move along,
Illumined through mist.

I hear something familiar in their wake...
Will my heart awake now?
Will I imagine new or old life's answer
Or both at the same time?

If the clouds were bringing evil,
My heart would not tremble...
The door creaked. My hand trembled.
Tears. And songs. And laments.
(*3 November 1901*)

 62

A fire—white, yellow, red;
    Shouts and ringing in the distance;
You will not deceive me, vain alarm;
    I see lights on the river.

9 The subject is feminine.

[74]

With this bright fire and late-night shouts
　　You will not destroy my dreams.
The phantom is gazing with enormous eyes
　　From out of human vanity.

Your death would do no more than to comfort my gaze,
　　And so burn your ships!
Here they are—quiet, luminous, rapid—
　　Rushing toward me from afar.
(*6 November 1901*)

Ascending the first steps,
I looked at the lineaments of the earth.
The days faded—the fits of frenzy
Were extinguished in the rosy distances.
But still tormented and burning with desire,
My spirit wept—and in the stellar depths
The sea of fire spread apart;
Someone's dream was whispering about me...
(*8 November 1901*)

A single impulse—impotent and tearful;
A single dream—weak in its excessiveness;
And again the dream, burning to the point of pain—
The powerless dream of a slave.
But taste the sorcery of daily woes
And another dream—the accursed dream of the ages.
In the crucible of souls' maturities
Blossoms the rapture of the gods.
(*17 November 1901*)

Whether it is I who write or whether from out of the grave
    You have sent your youth—
With the former roses the phantom dear to me
    I, as before, will entwine.

If I die, the birds of passage
    Will scatter the phantom, joking.
You too will say, leafing through the pages:
    "He was a child of God."
(*21 November 1901*)

I await the cold day,
It is the gray twilight I await.
My heart grew still, ringing:
You said: "I will come—

Await me at the crossroads—far from
Busy peopled streets
So that with the grandeur of the earth
You could not part.

 I will come quietly and be still
Like your heart, ringing.
I will open the doors for you
In the twilight of the winter day."
(*21 November 1901*)

You are waiting passionately. You are being called—
But I do not recognize the voices.
The hearth has cooled—your haven
Is the native steppe. Only there are you at home.

In the steppe are darkening distances,
Mists, phantoms, visions.
I like disturbance and sorrow,
You like repose and reconciliation.

Oh, how pitiful I am before you!
I embrace all, possess all,
Wishing to possess only you,
But I cannot and do not know how to!
(*22 November 1901*)

The day will come when a great thing will be achieved:
I foresee in the future an exploit of the soul.

You—different, mute, faceless—
Are hiding and telling fortunes in your concealment.

But what you will turn into, I do not know;
And you do not know if I will be yours,

While There people are celebrating a victory
Over a unitary and terrifying soul.
(*23 November 1901*)

I waited long—you came out late
But in my waiting my spirit was awakened.
Twilight was spreading, but tearlessly
I exerted myself to see and to hear.

When the first flame burst forth
And the word flew up to heaven—

The ice broke, the last stone fell,
And my heart caught fire.

You in the white blizzard, in the snowy moan,
Again floated up like a sorceress
And in the eternal light, in the eternal ringing,
The cupolas of the churches blended together.
(*27 November 1901*)

 70

Last night the snowy blizzard
Covered the footprints,
The gentle rosy
Morning is awakened by the light.

A red dawn rose,
Shining on the snow.
Bright and passionate,
It rocked the shore.

After the blue ice-floe
At midday I will float.
I will meet the frost-covered
Maiden in waking life.
(*5 December 1901*)

 71

It is dark in the rooms and stifling—
Go out at night, this starry night,
And admire indifferently
The hearts burning above the abyss.

Their bonfires are visible from afar,
Illuminating the surrounding darkness.

Their dreams are insatiable,
Excessive, unknown…

Oh, why in the nocturnal shining
Do they not fly above the abyss?
Why do they never fuse their
Desires in the sphere above the stars?
(*11 December 1901*)

72

*All the doors are locked and the jailer*
*Gave the keys to your merciless empress.*
Petrarch

The battle makes my heart rejoice:
I feel the freshness of military luxuriance
But the heat of the enemy's cheeks
Throws me into belated flight.

The new captivity is dearer than ever to me.
I gaze into the pitch-black dusk
But into the long coldness of these rooms
A wondrous guard sometimes descends.

He bewings and carries off
And illumines and makes misty
And his words flow sweetly
But every sound of them wounds my heart.

In him lies the secret of youth
And with a slow and sweet poison
He gently drugs the prisoner,
Bewitching him with his bottomless gaze.
(*15 December 1901*)

73

The annoying white one, gazing into
The frosty night, blocks my way.
I go straight toward him in deep alarm
And he, staggering, moves aside.

I can't overpower the frosty wonder...
Alongside him there grows in the distance—
Where a pile of rocks rises—
The sky-blue empress of earth.

And the empress stands in prayer and alarm,
Betrothed to the coldness of winter...
He, lifeless, stands on the road
And I, tormented by immortality, walk toward him.

But the immortal powers are in vain
And the empress does not regret loss of freedom...
Celebrating the victory of the grave,
The white one gazes into the frosty distances.
(*16 December 1901*)

74

Be silent as in the past, hiding the light—
I am not expecting early secrets.
My question has one answer:
Seek your star.

I am not expecting early secrets, believe me.
They will ascend not for me.
Before me the door to the secret
Refuge is closed.

Before me is the severe heat
Of the soul's tears and woes,

And on my soul is a fire—
One answer, one.

Be silent as in the past—I will track
The ascent of my star.
But to my heart, to my heart I will point out
The tracks of late secrets.

But others will dream of
The light of your spring's first secrets.
Our two waves will merge
In the crucible of late woes.
(*18 December 1901*)

 75

The growing dusk, believe me,
Reminded me of your unclear answer.
I am waiting—the door will suddenly open
And the disappearing light will rush in.
Like pale dreams in the past,
I remember the features of your face
And fragments of unfamiliar words
Like responses of former worlds
Where you lived and, pale, walked,
Hiding the dusk beneath your eyelashes,
And behind you a living boat,
Like a white swan, sailed
And behind the boat were streams of fire—
My agitated songs...
You listened to them pensively
And I remember the features of your face
And the pale heights
In which the last dreams soared.
In those heights I live, believe me,
By the obscure memory of those years of dusk.

I obscurely remember—the door will open
And the disappearing light will rush in.
(*20 December 1901*)

The dusk brings sadness.
The sleepy outline of dim streets,
The city, obscurely illumined,
Gazes into the rosy distances.

The capital's hopeless eye
Gazes from the gloomy earth:
The darkness has raised its eyes,
Angels soar in the distance.

The flaming dawn is at hand;
After the long night the morning
Will look into the corpse's eyes...
But the barely glimmering light flees

And the angels hide their frightened
Faces in their wings:
They see that a dead faceless one
Is growing in their rays.
(*24 December 1901*)

The old year carries away the dreams
Of untroubled blossoming.
At the dawn of another spring
The desired answer does not come.

The new year came at night
And spread its covers over us.

Someone's rays are stealing in,
Something in the heart is sounding.

The old year is going away.
With an incoherent plea,
Cruel girl, I will send
The northern night after you.

I will mist over with passion the dreams
Of untroubled blossoming.
The first day of your spring
Will be the fiery summer...
(*25 December 1901*)

### 78
### *To My Double*

You have achieved a difficult feat with regard to her,
But—poor friend!—have you discerned
Her attire, festive and wondrous,
And the strange spring flowers?...

I have waited for you. Your shadow flitted
In the distance, in the fields, where I too walked,
Where she too rested sometimes,
Where you sighed over the mysteries of being...

And did you know that I would triumph?
That you would disappear, achieving but not loving?
That I would find the insanely young dream
In the bloody flowers without you?
I need neither you nor your deeds.
To me you are ridiculous and pitiful, old man!
Your feat is mine as is your reward:
Insane laughter and crazy screams!
(*27 December 1901*)

## 79

We, two elders, are roaming in solitude;
A damp murk has spread around us.
Ahead of us are distant windows;
The blue distances are filled with light.

But from where does the blue light
Gaze and gaze into the mysterious darkness?
We tremble with a unique dream,
O unfathomable, before you.

Oh, from where, from where did
The dark clouds turn red, burning?
From where do the golden threads run
And from where does the dawn redden the darkness?

We, two elders, are roaming into the mysterious
Darkness—but there is light in the windows.
And we tremble with a unique dream,
Tested by the wisdom of woes.
(*29 December 1901*)

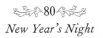

## 80
### New Year's Night

Cold mists are spreading;
Crimson bonfires are burning.
Svetlana's[10] frosty soul

---

10  The heroine of Zhukovsky's' ballad "Svetlana (1813)," which takes place on the
Eve of Epiphany, when girls traditionally tell their fortunes with regard to love and mar-
riage. Svetlana is expecting her beloved to return home when a woman persuades her to
take part in the fortune telling. She dreams of seeing him and together "...gallop[ing]
across the snowy midnight fields in a sleigh, passing churches and peasant huts." Then,
when she walks into one of the huts, she sees a corpse that struggles to rise from the cof-
fin to seize her; the corpse turns out to be her betrothed. The dream obviously troubles
Svetlana, because she fears that her beloved has died. However, the next day, he returns
home safely. In Blok's poem Svetlana is conflated with Liubov Dmitrievna Mendeeleva.

Is lost in the dreams of a mysterious game.
   A sleigh scrapes through the snow, hearts start stirring,
   The gentle moon comes out again.
   Beyond the gates people laugh;
   Further on, the street is dark.
   Let me glance at the holiday of laughter;
   I will come down, my face covered!
   The red ribbons are so pretty,
   My darling looks to see what's doing on the porch...
   But the mist does not stir,
   I await the midnight hour.
   Someone whispers and laughs
   And the bonfires burn and burn...
   A sleigh scrapes through the snow; in the frosty distances
   A gentle light steals up on you.
   Someone's sleigh dashes past...
   "Your name?" Laughter in response...
   A snowy whirlwind rises,
   Whitening the whole porch...
   And my laughing and tender darling
   Covers my face...

Cold mists are spreading,
Turning pale, the moon steals up on you.
Pensive Svetlana's soul
Is troubled by a wondrous dream...
(*31 December 1901*)

# IV

 81

I was walking—and behind me walked
Some sort of frenzied people.
Their hair stood on end under the moon;
In terror, with tormented souls
They gnashed their teeth and beat their breasts,
And the sound of their gnashing was borne afar.

I was walking—and behind me dragged
Weary, pensive people.
They had forgotten the fateful terror.
Their sunken, tortured breasts
Tranquilly inhaled the nocturnal aroma
And their arms were lifelessly intertwined.

Ahead of me went a pillar of fire.
And I counted the steps of enormous crowds.
And their gnashing and their idle rustle
Were observed by me, boundless and happy.
(*1 January 1902*)

 82
*To S. Solovyov*

Uncertain daytime shadows are racing.
High and distinct is the call of the bells.
The church steps are illuminated,
Their stone is alive—and awaits your steps.

You will pass by here and touch the cold stone,
Garbed in the terrible holiness of the ages,

[86]

And perhaps you will drop a springtime flower
Here, in this darkness, in front of the severe icons.

The rosy shadows are growing indistinctly.
High and distinct is the call of the bells.
Darkness spreads over the old steps...
I am illuminated—I await your steps.
(*4 January 1902*)

 83

The darkness of the church vestibule would intensify
On days of weddings, on days of births and of funerals;
And over there a wide road meandered
And a pilgrim walked, illumined by the sunset.

Over there the open expanses were endless
But here, in the shadows, you couldn't see a thing;
And every time the passerby would encounter
Answering steps from the darkness.

With its measured ringing the church vault
Would send off every pilgrim on his way,
And in the depths, above the dark ambo,[11]
A warning light would be streaming.

And before passing into the laughing distances,
The pilgrim would wait, pensive and embarrassed,
For the light to fade and the sounds to stop...
And then he would walk on, illumined by the sunset.
(*4 January 1902*)

---

11  In old Orthodox churches, the ambo was a raised platform in the middle of the
nave from which the scriptures were read during the Divine Liturgy.

84

High above, the wall merges with the darkness;
A luminous window and luminous silence.
Not a sound at the door, the stairs are dark,
And a familiar trembling roams about the corners.

A trembling light in the doorway and twilight all around.
Immense commotion and noise on the street.
I am silent and await you, my poor, delayed friend,
The last dream of my evening soul.
(*11 January 1902*)

85

Over there, in the half-darkness of the cathedral,
In the light of an icon's lamp,
The living night will soon gaze
Into your sleepless eyes.

In the speeches about heavenly wisdom
You sense earthly currents.
Up there, beneath the arches, you find unknown darkness,
While here you have the coldness of a stone bench.

The intense heat of an accidental meeting
Breathed from the church heights
Onto these slumbering candles,
Onto the icons and the flowers.

The silence is inspiring,
Your thoughts are hidden,
And you obscurely sense the knowledge
And the trembling of the dove and of the serpent.
(*14 January 1902*)

We bowed down before the scriptures
And were taken aback by the silence of the temple.
In the rays of the divine light
The smile of the Woman was remembered.

Souls united and silent,
In the same rays and within the same walls,
We perceived the solar waves
Above—on the dark cupolas.

And from that ancient gilding,
From those terrible depths,
Onto my holiday descended Someone
With the smile of the tender Woman.
(*18 January 1902, St. Isaac's Cathedral*)

I am hidden for a while in the chapel
But large wings are growing.
The hour will come—all thought of the body will disappear
And the heights will become transparent and luminous.

As luminous as on the day of our joyful meeting,
As transparent as your dream.
You will hear my sweet speeches,
My lips will bloom with new power.

Before you and I had time to ascend—
My heavy shield caught fire.
Solitary, let it now in the fateful chapel
Burn to the end in my heart.

I will raise a new shield for our meeting,
I will lift up my living heart again.

You will hear my sweet speeches,
You will respond to my love.

The hour will come—into the cold blizzards
The distances of spring will gaze, merry.
I am hidden for a while in the chapel
But all-powerful wings are growing.
(*29 January 1902*)

 88

We will not long admire
These earthly feasts:
 Before us mysteries will be bared
And distant worlds will shine forth.
(*January 1902*)

 89

The day is ending. The last rays
Burn in the dust of the road.
Their red reflection has merged into one
With my candle's flame.

And my night, leisurely clear,
Sails on toward another night.
I may not notice the red reflection—
But it will surely come.

And all that was impossible
In the alarms of the day or in the morning,
Will come to pass here, in the dust of the road,
In the rays of sunset, as evening approaches.
(*1 February 1902*)

90

Dreams of strange reflections
Lie in wait during my day.
Here is the flaming shadow
Of belated visions.

All the rays of my freedom
Reddened there.
Here, snows and tempests
Have encircled the temple.

All the visions are so momentary—
Should I believe in them?
But the Empress of the universe,
Ineffable beauty,
Perhaps loves me,
Accidental, poor, perishable.

Days of meetings, days of reflections
Lie in wait in the stillness...
Should I expect the fiery madness
Of a young soul?

Or, frozen in the snowy temple,
Not baring my face,
Should I greet with conjugal gifts
The messengers of the end?
(*3 February 1902*)

 91

To the springtime holiday of light
I invite a dear shadow.
Come, do not wait for dawn;
Bring day with you!

There is a new day—not the one that with the wind
Beats on the windows in the springtime!
Let this unprecedented day laugh
Ceaselessly at the window!

We will open the doors then,
Weep, and sigh;
Our winter losses
With a light heart we will bear...
(*3 February 1902*)

 92

You were strangely luminous
And, with your smile, not simple.
In the rays of your darkness
I understood the young Christ.
A bright unearthly reflection
Pierced the former clouds.
We are rocked tranquilly
By the emerald wave.
Your loving caress illuminates
Me—and I see dreams.
But, believe me, I think the unprecedented sign
Of spring is something fabulous.
(*8 February 1902*)

 93

People without sorrow won't understand
These masks and this laughter at the window!
At crossroads I seek the absence of people;
Entertainments are not for me!

Oh, strangely sweet are the tunes...
They seem so clear!

And here the pale maidens
Have already prepared the way for spring.

They know what is unknown to me,
But now only one is singing...
I have been ardently tracking her
All night, all night—at the window!
(*10 February 1902*)

## 94

*For the sun there is no return.*
(*From Ostrovsky's* Snow Maiden)

The dreams are obscure, the colors are vivid;
I do not feel sorry for the pale stars.
Look at how the solar caresses
In the azure coddle the stern cross.

So—to these caresses at sunset
The cross gives itself, as do we,
Because "for the sun there is no return"
From the approaching darkness.

The sun will set and, growing still,
We too will have our repose and the cross will fade—
And then we will awaken again, withdrawing
Into the calm coldness of the pale stars.
(*12 February 1902*)

## 95

We live in an ancient cell
    In a region of floods.
The spring is full of merriment here
    And the river sings.

But as a harbinger of the merriments,
    On days of springtime storms,
Through the doors of our cells will pour
    Luminous azure.

And full of the sacred awe
    Of long-awaited years,
We will rush toward a pathless place
    Into indescribable light.
(*18 February 1902*)

 96

*And the Spirit and the Bride say, Come.*
Revelation 22:7

I believe in the Sun of the Testament,
I see dawns in the distance.
I await universal light
From the springtime earth.

All that is full of falsehood
Has been thrown back, trembling.
Before me, toward pathlessness,
Is a region of gold.

I pass through forests
Of forbidden lilies.
Angels' wings fill
The heavens above me.

Streams of unfathomable
Light tremble.
I believe in the Sun of the Testament,
I see Your eyes.
(*22 February 1902*)

97

Someone is whispering with God
    At the holy icon.
The mystery of life is gleaming,
    The annunciating bells are ringing.
Immaculateness is knocking
    At the doors of God's spirit.
The heart is transported
    Into pathless distances.
Here—I make my vows
    Of wisdom of humility.[12]
In vestments of chastity,
    O holy maiden, where are you?
Wearied by trials,
    I await You,
Tender, dear,
    Ever young.
(*27 February 1902*)

98

We will forgive everything—and not disturb
The peace of the maidens of spring;
We will put out the divine fire
And chase away the tender dreams.

There are no limits to our knowledge,
The material temple is not eternal.
When we were erecting the building,
We dreamt that it would fall.

And every time we entered beneath the vaults,
Praying and weeping, we knew:

12  An Orthodox monastic practice whereby the practitioner seeks to be "deified"
through the extreme humbling of himself.

Wild winds would blow through
And the snows of winter would cover everything.
(*February 1902*)

 99

You are God's day. My dreams
Are eagles screaming in the azure.
Under the wrath of radiant beauty
They are ceaselessly in the whirlwind of the storm.

The arrow pierces their hearts,
They fly in wild free-fall...
But even in their fall there is no end
To the praise or to the shrieks and screams!
(*21 February 1902*)

 100

All day before me,
Young and golden,
Flooded with bright sunlight,
You walked on your bright road.

Merging with the dear, distant one,
That is how I spent the spring day,
And I went without sadness
To meet the luminous evening shadow.

The blissful days' dream—
You walked on your pure road.
O, appear before me
Not in my imagination alone!
(*February 1902*)

101

Over there the twilight trembled,
Mysteriously taking the place of the empty day.
Who, passing by, enslaved my soul's stone tablets
By an obstinate dream?

Who, passing by, anxiously cast glances
At this obscurely departing day?
Over there, in the depths, dreams and thoughts pass rapidly,
While here on earth both light and shadow are like a dream.

But I will understand and embrace everything with dream,
I will cast aside sleep and see things in waking reality.
The one who touched here the same earth as I,
After him into the evening twilight I will sail.
(*February 1902*)

 102

I and He wandered through cities.
Sleepy people looked at us from windows.
I walked in front, and behind me walked He Himself,
All-penetrating and close to the goal.

I was afraid of my involuntary powers,
He directed my enchanted step.
Sometimes a passerby would walk close by
And secretly tremble, dismayed...

People would see us in black cities
And, sleepy, would look at us trustingly:
I walked in front, but behind me walked He Himself,
Similar to me. But close to the goal.
(*February 1902*)

103

Conjure and wait. In the middle of the night,
In your window, dear friend,
Bold eyes will light up
And the agreed-on knock will be heard.

And blowing out the candles,
He, like some Spirit, covering his face
And with the hope of an impossible rendezvous,
Will enter the dear porch.
(*15 March 1902*)

104

Slow life was passing like an old fortune teller
Mysteriously whispering forgotten words.
I was sighing over something, feeling sorry for something;
My head was burning with some reverie.

Stopping at a crossroads in the field,
I gazed at the jagged woods.
But even here, under the yoke of an alien will,
The sky seemed heavy.

And I remembered the hidden causes
Of the enslavement of my thoughts and my young powers.
And over there, in the distance, the departing day
Was languidly gilding the tops of the jagged woods.

Spring, spring! Tell me, what do I feel sorry for?
What reverie is burning my head?
Mysteriously, like an old fortune teller,
Life is whispering forgotten words to me.
(*16 March 1902*)

## 105

My evening is near and without will.
The heavens acquire an evening tinge—
Sounds emanate from the bell towers,
I hear the voices of winged beings.

With your caressing and subtle sting
You probe my depths;
I track with weary vision
The coming of a spring so alien to me.

Between us there is accidental agitation.
An accidentally sweet deception
Has doomed me to veneration
And summoned you out of white lands.

And infinitely distant,
The voices will stop sorrowfully
When, wrapped in shadow,
My heavens fade.
( *27 March 1902* )

## 106

In the dark vestibule I whisper
Saintly names on the sly.
I know: there are two of us in the temple.
You think: you are alone…

I listen to your sighs
In some sort of unrealizable dream…
Words about some sort of love…
And—O God!—reveries about me…

But again there is silence all around
And the weeping voice has stopped…

And again I whisper insanely
The names of forgotten saints.

All is illusion, all is sorrow, all is falsehood!
I tremble, pray, and whisper...
O, if you extend your wings to fly,
I will fly away with you forever!...
(*March 1902*)

 107

I was slowly losing my mind
At the door of the one I long for.
The spring day was changing into darkness,
Which only heightened my longing.

I wept, wearied by passion,
And gloomily suppressed my moans.
A sick insane thought, festering,
Was already splitting in two.

And it penetrated into the quietude
Of my soul, already insane,
And flooded my spring
With a noiseless black wave.

The spring day was changing into darkness,
My heart was turning cold over the grave.
I was slowly losing my mind,
I was thinking coldly about my darling.
(*March 1902*)

 108

The spring is breaking the ice floes in the river
And I feel no sorrow over my dear dead ones:

Having climbed to my peaks,
I have forgotten the winter ravines
And see the sky-blue distances.

Why have regrets in the smoke of the fire,
Why feel agony before the cross,
When I ceaselessly await the blow
Or the divine gift
From Moses' bush!
(*March 1902*)

109

Who is weeping here? Onto the peaceful steps
All should ascend—and enter through the open gates.
There—in the interior—Mary awaits your prayers,
Renewed by Christ's birth.

Fortifying your spirit by the hope for a higher destiny,
You, too, should enter, sorrowing woman.
Your beloved fell, but the news in the bloody field,
The news of Love, is as clear as before.

There is no place here for the victory of pitiful corruptions;
Here all is love. Through the open gates
All should enter. Mary awaits your prayers,
Renewed by Christ's birth.
(*March 1902*)

110

Weary, I was losing hope
And being overcome by dark anguish.
Your pure garments shone white,
Your gentle hand trembled.

"Is it you who are here? The valley has sunk
Into a sleep without waking...
You descended, touched me, and sighed.
Is tomorrow the day of freedom for me?"

"I have descended and will be with you until the morning;
At dawn I will leave your dream,
Vanish without a trace, and forget everything;
And you will awake, free again."
(*1 April 1902*)

111

I seek strange and new things on the pages
Of old and familiar books;
I dream of white vanished birds
And sense the isolated instant.

Agitated rudely by the commotion of life
And dismayed by whispers and shouts,
I am anchored securely by my white dream
To the shore of the recent past.

White You are, imperturbable in the depths,
Stern and wrathful in life,
Mysteriously anxious and mysteriously loved,
Maiden, Dawn, Burning Bush.

The cheeks of golden-haired maidens fade,
Dawns are not as eternal as dreams.
Thorns crown the humble and wise
With the white fire of the Burning Bush.
(*4 April 1902*)

112

In the daytime I enact works of vanity,
In the evening I light candles.
Inexorably unfathomable, you
Play games with me.

I love this falsehood, this glitter,
Your alluring maidenly attire,
The eternal hubbub and the commotion of the streets,
The receding row of street lamps.

I love, admire, and await
Your iridescent colors and words.
I will approach and then again withdraw
Into the depths of my ongoing dreams.

How false you are and how white!
I love white falsehood…
As I finish my daytime works,
I know in the evening you will come again.
(*5 April 1902*)

113

I love, humbling my soul,
To visit tall cathedrals,
To enter the twilight-hidden choir
And disappear in the crowd of singers.
I fear my two-faced soul
And am careful to encase
My devilish and savage aspect
In this holy armor.
In my superstitious prayer
I seek protection from Christ,
But beneath my hypocritical mask
My lying lips are laughing.

And quietly, with changed face,
In the dead glimmer of the candles,
I awake the memory of the Two-Faced one
In the hearts of the praying people.
But—the choir trembles and stops singing,
And everyone starts to run in panic...
I love, humbling my soul,
To visit tall cathedrals.
(*8 April 1902*)

114

I know the day of my curses
And flee to my premature monastery;
I tear myself from his embrace
But he lies in wait for me at the crossroads.

His noisome shouts,
Sometimes near, sometimes distant,
And fear, and shame, and savage terror,
And naked anguish.

And at the crossroads, a pitiful captive,
I stumble and scream...
He lures me with a white mermaid,
In the distance he holds a glimmering candle...

And weary with torment and in a frenzy,
I return into the world—
To endless agony,
To endless love.
(*13 April 1902*)

115

We withdrew and stood at the helm
Where silvery streams went past
And we observed the raised sail,
The evening of the day, and your lines.

Disappearing in the dusk, you fearlessly
Controlled the wind on the rapids.
You, like the sunset, were fading darkly
In his soul—and were singing about me.

And, blissful at the wheel, I measured
Every sound, both short and long,
While he looked on, pensive and dignified,
As in the distance the earth grew dark...
(*13 April 1902*)

116

I am a trembling creature. Illumined
By beams of light, my dreams stagnate.
Compared to Your depths
My depths are negligible.
Do You not know what goals
You conceal in the depths of Your Roses,
What angels have flown down,
Who stands hushed at the threshold...
In You is concealed the expectation
Of great light and of evil darkness—
The unriddling of all knowledge
And the delirium of a great mind.
(*26 April 1902*)

## ❧ 117 ❧

I hear the church bell. In the field it is spring.
You have opened the gay windows.
The day was laughing and fading. Alone, you tracked
The rosy filaments of the clouds.
The laughter passed over your face but stopped and disappeared...
What was it that went by and disconcerted you?
I am going away into the reddening woods...
You forgot me as soon as you said goodbye.
(*April 1902*)

## ❧ 118 ❧

Over there in the street there was a nondescript house
With steep stairs leading into darkness.
The door would open with a ringing of glass;
The light would rush out—and the darkness would start roaming
    again.

There in the twilight you could see an awning
Bolted to the door under a sign that said "Flowers."
There the rattle of steps would fade and cease
On the stairs under the yellow light of a lamp.

There, up above, a window looked down,
Veiled by immobile blinds,
And like a knitted brow the ledge
Imparted a grimace to the wall—as well as gazes...

There, in the twilight, a light quivered in the windows
And there were singing, music, and dances.
But from the street you couldn't hear the words or sounds—
There was only the luster of the window glass.

On the stairs above the dark yard
A shadow trembled and the lamp glowed dimly.

Suddenly the door would open with a ringing of glass;
The light would rush out, and the darkness would start roaming again.
(*1 May 1902*)

I and the world—snow, streams,
The sun, songs, stars, birds,
Swarms of confused thoughts—
All are Your subjects, all are Yours!

We are not afraid of everlasting captivity
And do not notice the narrowness of the walls.
From limit to limit
Sufficient is that we shudder,
That we undergo change!

To love, to hate
The universe's hidden meaning,
The odd and even of dead numbers,
And up above—to see You!
(*10 May 1902*)

You and I would meet at sunset,
You'd cleave the bay with your oar.
I loved your white dress,
Having stopped loving the exquisiteness of the dream.

Our wordless meetings were strange.
Up ahead—on the sandy spit—
Evening candles were lit.
Someone was thinking of the pale beauty.

The approaches, the closenesses, the burnings
Are not accepted by the azure stillness...
We met in the evening mist
In a place of ripples and reeds at the shore.

No anguish, no love, no injury;
It has all faded, passed, receded...
Your white figure, the voices of the requiem,
And your golden oar.
(*13 May 1902*)

121

You were hidden in mists
And even your voice was weak.
I remember those deceptions,
I remember them, your obedient slave.

You wore a crown
Of dawn caprices.
I remember the steps of your throne
And your first severe judgment.

What pale dresses!
What strange stillness!
And arms full of lilies
And your gaze bereft of thought...

Who knows where this was?
 Where did the Star fall?
What words did you speak
And did you speak at all then?

But how could I not recognize
The white river flower
And those white dresses
And the strange white hint?
(*May 1902*)

When all around is the motionless stillness
Of holy forgetfulness,
You gaze in quiet languor,
Having spread apart the river reeds.

I love those green grasses
Even on sleepy days.
Do they not contain my hidden,
My golden fires?

You gaze, quiet and stern,
Into the eyes of the departed dream.
I have chosen another road;
I am on it—and the songs are not the same...

Soon evening will come
And then night—to meet fate:
Then my path will be reversed
And I will return to You.
(*May 1902*)

You did not go away. But perhaps
In your unfathomable way
You were able to exhaust and expel
All the things of earth I love...

And there is no parting more difficult:
To you, an unanswering rose,
I sing, a gray nightingale
Caged in my multicolored prison!
(*28 May 1902*)

# V

 124

I roam within the walls of a monastery,
A joyless and dark monk.
The pale dawn barely glimmers—
I track the fluttering of snowflakes.

O, the night is long, the dawn is pale
In our somber north.
At the snowed-in window
I abandon myself to stubborn thoughts.

The same old snow—whiter than
An untouched and eternal vestment.
And the eternally pale wax of the candles
And the whitened window ledges.

Strange to me is the coldness of these walls
And incomprehensible is the poverty of this life.
I am frightened by the sleepy captivity
And by the brothers' deathly paleness.

The dawn is pale and the night is long,
Like the series of matins and liturgies.
O, I myself am as pale as the snow;
With all my stubborn thought, my heart is poor…
(*11 June 1902, Shakhmatovo*)

 125

I open the shutters on their rusty loops
And breathe the first sweet currents.
The mist has descended from the mountain
And, white, it has enveloped my demesne.

It has grown light there but the sun has not yet risen.
I sense expectation all around.
May your sleep be untroubled. You were not awakened
By my reverie, my tranquil friend.

A pensive dreamer, I cannot sleep:
At the head of the bed, in a mysterious conjuration,
I, a philosopher and sculptor, will portray
Your features and convey them to you.

At some future time in a moment of rapture,
When you are alone with him at sunset,
You will present your portrait to him
And say casually: "How he loved me!"
(*June 1902*)

 126

The golden-haired angel of the day
Will turn into a night fairy
But she too will go away, ringing,
When the momentary dream is dreamt.

We are bounded by the blue azure
And by the womb of mother earth.
Within those bounds stillness is the harbinger of storms
And storms are messengers of tranquility.

As long as you are alive, there is one law
For infant, sage, and maiden.
Why, mortal, are you dismayed
By the criminal dream of divine wrath?
(*Summer 1902*)

 127

She broke through in a singing stream,
Departed into the mute azure,
Disappeared in the deep expanses
As a distant dreaming of storms.
We, forgotten in the waste land,
Lived in our poverty, bereft of tears,
Trembled, prayed toward the cliffs,
Did not see the burning roses.
Suddenly she flew into our somber north,
Appeared in her astonishing beauty,
Called herself the thought of death,[13]
With sun, moon, and stars in her scythe.
The clouds withdrew in alarm,
Everyday life was enshrouded in sweet darkness,
Holy roads were formed
As if heaven had returned to the earth.
And in our waste land
We apprehended the burning of the roses.
Our evil thoughts and the proud cliffs—
All melted away in a flame of tears.
(*1 July 1902*)

128
*On the Death of My Grandfather*
(1 July 1902)[14]

We waited together for death or sleep.
Instants of torment went by.
Suddenly a breeze came through the window,
A page of the Holy Book stirred.

13 Blok's beloved grandfather, A. N. Beketov, died in Shakhmatovo on the day of the writing of this poem.
14 See previous footnote.

An elder walked there, hoary with age,
With bold step and gay eyes;
He laughed to us and beckoned with his hand,
And went away with a familiar walk.

And suddenly all of us there—old and young—
Recognized in him the one who lay before us,
And tremulously turning around,
We saw the deceased with closed eyes…

But it was sweet to follow his soul
And to see gaiety in its departure.
Our hour had come to remember and to love,
And to celebrate a different kind of housewarming.
(*Shakhmatovo*)

 129

Do not be afraid to die on the road.
Fear neither enemies nor friends.
Attend to the words of the service
In order to transcend the bounds of fear.

She will descend to you herself.
In slavery to corruption you will no longer
Beckon the laughing sunrise
In poor and humble form.

She and you are one law,
One command of the Higher Will.
You are not doomed forever
To hopeless and deathly pain.
(*5 July 1902*)

130

*He that hath the bride is the bridegroom: but the friend of the*
*bridegroom, which standeth and heareth him, rejoiceth*
*greatly because of the bridegroom's voice...*
John 3:29

I, a youth, light the candles
And guard the censer's fire.
She, thoughtless and wordless,
Laughs on the other shore.

I love the evening prayer
In the white church above the river,
The village before sunset,
And the dark-blue twilight.

Captivated by her tender glances,
I admire her mysterious beauty
And throw white flowers
Over the church fence.

The dark curtain will fall.
The bridegroom will descend from the sanctuary
And from the peaks of the jagged woods
A conjugal dawn will glimmer.
(*7 July 1902*)

131

They uttered brief speeches,
Toward evening they awaited strange news.
No one came out to meet me.
I stood alone at the door.

Many came up to the house,
Screaming and sobbing violently.
I was not acquainted with any of them
And I was not moved by their appearance.

They were all waiting for some sort of news.
From fragments of words I made out
Some crazy ravings about a bride
And that someone had run away.

And having ascended the hill beyond the garden,
They were all gazing into the blue distances.
And with insincere looks on their faces
They all tried to show sorrow.

I alone did not go away from the door
And did not dare to enter and ask.
It was sweet to know about the loss
But ridiculous to talk about it.

So I stood alone—without agitation.
I gazed at the mountains in the distance.
And there—on the steep road—
Red dust was already swirling.
(*15 July 1902*)

 132

I ran down from the mountain and stood still in the thicket.
Lanterns are glimmering all around…
How my heart is beating—ever more spitefully and violently!…
They will keep searching for me until dawn.

They are not familiar with swamp lights.
My eyes are the eyes of an owl.
Let them track me, running,
Through the twisted grass.

My swamp will suck them in.
The muddy ring will close

And, turning upside down, my white phantom
Will gaze into their faces.
(*21 July 1902*)

 133

I am young and fresh and in love;
I am anxious, anguished, and in prayer;
I, mysterious maple, grow green,
Constantly turned toward you.
The warm wind will pass through my leaves—
My trunks will tremble from prayer;
On my face, turned toward the stars,
Are aromatic tears of praise.
You will come under my broad canopy
On these pale sleepy days
To admire my dear attire
And to dream in the green shade.
You are alone, in love and with me;
I will whisper a mysterious dream;
And until the night—I am with anguish and with you;
I, greening maple, am with you.
(*31 July 1902*)

 134

Terrible is the cold of evenings;
Their wind, flailing in alarm;
The worrying rustle of
Nonexistent footsteps on the road.

This cold feature of the sunset
Is like the memory of a recent illness
And a sure sign that we are trapped
Inside a circle that will never open.
(*July 1902*)

[116]

135

The white ice vanished
Beyond the dark city distances.
I became friends with the darkness
And walked less rapidly.

There was a roar from the black heights
And snow was falling.
A man rose toward me
Out of the darkness.

Hiding his face from me,
He walked rapidly ahead
Toward where there were no lights
And where the ice ended.

He turned around—I encountered
One burning eye.
Then the polynya[15] was closed off—
His fire had gone out.

The frosty ring merged
Into a gentle jetlike flow.
The tender face turned red,
The cold snow sighed.

And I did not know when and where
He had appeared and disappeared—
When the azure dream of the heavens
Turned upside down in the water...
(*4 August 1902*)

---

15  Unfrozen patch of water in the midst of an ice-bound river.

136

The light in the window was swaying.
In the half-darkness a harlequin,
Alone in the doorway,
Was whispering to the darkness.

His white and red costume
Was enveloped in darkness.
Above—on the other side of the wall—
A clownish masquerade was going on.

The people there covered their faces
With multicolored falsehood.
But in their hands they recognized
An inevitable shaking.

*He* wrote something on the ground
With a wooden sword.
*She*, enraptured by this strange
Act, dropped her eyes.

Not believing in rapture,
Alone with the darkness,
The harlequin was laughing
At the pensive door.
(*6 August 1902*)

 137

I tried to rest my heart—
Could I not cast off those dreams?
But someone was waiting at the crossroads
For my last, terrifying words.

He is still waiting. The shadows are waning.
Clearer and nearer is the dream of the end.

He has hidden his head in his knees
And does not show me his face.

But on the last day, in the bottomless hour,
Having violated every possible law,
He will rise, a lawless phantom,
Reflected by the mirror-like surfaces.

And in that hour into the empty entryway
Will enter the likeness of a face,
And in the mirror without shadow
One will see the image of the visitor.
(*27 August 1902*)

138

Through a golden valley
You are departing, silent and strange.
Fading in the sky is the receding
Cry of cranes.

It is as if a sad voice, a long sound,
Is frozen at the zenith.
An exultant spider
Infinitely draws forth its filaments.

Through the transparent filaments
The sun, not hiding its light,
Idly beats against the blind windows
Of the empty dwelling.

For its festive attire
Autumn has given to the sun
The vanished hopes
Of inspired heat.
(*29 August 1902*)

139

Without Me[16] your dreams would fly away
Into the murkily undesired heights;
You should remember the evening distances
And knock, my child, at the door of my serene tower.

I live above the jagged earth
And spend the nights in My tower.
Come, I will give you peace;
Darling, darling, I will embrace you.

I have gone way into the snows without return
But, swirling the cold whirlwinds,
At the boundary of the fiery sunset
I have inscribed the Name, my child...
(*August 1902*)

 140

I will meet you somewhere in the world
Beyond the stone roads.
At the last dread feast
God is preparing a meeting for us.
(*August 1902*)

16  The subject is feminine.

# VI

 141

I went out into the night—to recognize, to understand
The distant rustle, the nearby noise,
To receive a nonexistent guest, to believe
In the truth of horse hoofs' imaginary clatter.

The road, white under the moon,
Seemed to be full of footsteps.
Someone's shadow was wandering there
And sank beyond the hills.

I listened—and heard:
Amid the trembling lunar spots,
Far away, a horse was galloping with hoofs ringing
And a light whistling was recognizable.

But here, and farther, there was a uniform sound
And my heart slowly struggled:
Oh, how can one understand where the clatter is coming from,
Where the voice will be coming from?

And now the ringing of the hoofs was more distinct
And a white horse was galloping toward me…
And it became clear who was silent
And laughing in the empty saddle.

I went out into the night—to recognize, to understand
The distant rustle, the nearby noise,
To receive a nonexistent guest, to believe
In the truth of horse hoofs' imaginary clatter.
(*6 September 1902, Petersburg*)

142

Joyless seeds are sprouting.
The cold wind beats against the bare twigs.
I have discovered certain writings in my soul.
I conceal them—in villages, at crossroads…
And I steal like a shadow along lunar walls.
The walls change, darken, grow wild with vegetation.
All change is sweet to me.
Every day gives birth to changes for me.
Oh, how alive I am, how powerful the flow of my blood is!
I am kindred here with subterranean flows!
Moments of mysteries! You, eternal love!
I have understood you! I am with you! I am for you!
The great wall is growing, growing.
The cold wind beats against the bare twigs…
I have discovered you, sacred writings.
And I guard you with a smile at the crossroads.
(*6 September 1902*)


143

A church bell rang in the city,
Praising my recent dreams.
I withdrew and prayed
Where I had seen You.

Listening to the call of someone of another faith
And filled with the memory of recent days,
My heart beat as before,
My soul had not changed.

All has withdrawn and betrayed me
And is whispering about my soul…
Only You have preserved
Your Ancient Mystery.
(*15 September 1902*)

144

I awoke and ascended
To the window on dark steps.
The frosty moon silvered
My quiet vestibule.

I long have had no news
But the city brought me its sounds
And every day I awaited guests
And listened to the rustling and knocks.

And at night I would repeatedly shudder
And, awakened by steps,
Would ascend to the window—and see
Rows of gas lamps glimmering in the streets.

Today I await my guests
And shudder and wring my hands.
I long have had no news
But there have been rustling and knocks.
(*18 September 1902*)

 145
*Ecclesiastes*[17]

Blessing light and darkness
And rejoicing in the music of the lyre,
Look there—into the unearthly chaos
Toward which your day declines.

Intact is the silver chain,
Your jugs are full,
The almond blossoms at the bottom of the valley,
And the steppe gives off moist heat.

17  This poem is based on Ecclesiastes 12:3-6.

[123]

You are going home over the mountains,
Drenched with the midday sun;
As you walk, a golden ribbon
Sinks in your pitch-black hair.

The capers' flowers have withered,
The grasshopper grows fat,
And on the road there is a sense of terror
And the heavens have turned dark.

The millstones have grown tired of milling,
The frightened sentries run away,
And all are seized by an enemy phantom
And the trees bend down to the ground.

Everything is gripped by a wild fear.
Men and beasts are crowded together.
And those who had been looking out the window
Vainly lock their doors.
(*24 September 1902*)

 146

She is stately and tall
And always haughty and severe.
Every day I, ready for anything,
Observed her from a distance.

I knew what hour she would descend
Together with her quivering radiance.
And, like a villain, I ran after her,
Playing hide and seek.

Yellow lights glimmered
Along with electric candles.
He would meet her in the shadows
And I observed and sang their meetings.

When, suddenly confused,
They'd sense something,
I'd hide behind
Some dark blind gate.

And I, unseen by all,
Would observe the man's rough profile
And her silvery black fur
And lips that whispered something.
(27 September 1902)

147

It was late evening, crimson;
The precursor star had risen.
Above the abyss a new voice was crying—
The Virgin had given birth to the Infant.

Following the thin lingering voice,
Like the long squeal of a spinning wheel,
There came in confusion an imposing elder,
A king, a youth, and a woman.

A sign and miracle appeared:
In the total stillness
In the midst of the crowd arose Judas
In a cold mask, on a horse.

The rulers, full of cares,
Sent the news to all the ends of the earth,
And on Iscariot's lips
The messengers saw a smile.
(*19 April–28 September 1902*)

### 148

### *The Old Man*
### To A.S.F.[18]

Having grown old and forgotten what is holy,
I live by cold attention.
There had recently been two of us,[19]
But that was in a dream, not in waking reality.

I look at the pale autumnal colors
And my memory whispers something to me...
But can one believe a shadow
That glimmered in a youthful dream?

Was all this real or did I only imagine it?
In hours when old wounds had been forgotten
I sometimes had long reveries
That have now disappeared in the mist.

But I, ill and under the yoke of gray hairs,
Do not believe in stupid fairy-tales.
Let others find the doors
That are not destined for me.
(*29 September 1902*)

### 149

Under the yellow light they made merry,
All night the circle grew tighter at the walls,
The rows of dancers doubled,
And I seemed to see my inseparable friend.

Desire lifted breasts,
Faces were hot.

18 Andrei Sergeevich Famintsyn (1835–1918), botanist and physiologist.
19 Allusion to A.S.F.'s close friend A.N. Beketov, who had died recently.

I passed by, dreaming of a miracle
And tortured by others' lust...

Over there, behind a haze of dust,
Hidden in the crowd, someone seemed to live,
And strange eyes observed,
And a voice sang and spoke...
(*September 1902*)

 150

Of legends, of fables, of mysteries.
There was one All-triumphant Christ.
He inscribed himself in deserts and in incidental
Thoughts and brought whirlwinds.

We were tortured and worn by the ages
And hardened our hearts with iron;
Weary, we again remembered
The unfathomable mystery of the Father.

And outstretched on the ground before him,
We know one thing with certainty:
The iron-tormented dream
Cannot understand the Golden Word.
(*September 1902*)

 151

He'd enter, plain and meager; he'd barely
Breathe, say nothing, and go out like a flame.
A laughing eye, emerald-like,
Would always be watching him.

Or secretly amazed,
It would gaze at him in the stillness.
He would say nothing, bewitched
By another soul's sweet nearness.

But, counting the instants, he knew
This soul would always betray him.
On the pages of the secret book
He saw the same sacred characters.

He was strange—a plain, meager,
Silent misanthrope.
Attentive and wondrous,
The secret eye kept watching him.
(*September 1902*)

152

He appeared at the elegant ball
In a brilliantly closed circle.
Sinister lights twinkled
And his gaze described an arc.

All night they went round in a noisy dance,
All night the circle grew tighter at the walls.
And at dawn in a glossy window
A noiseless friend appeared.

He got up and lifted his sleepy gaze,
Intently watching the pale
Columbine being chased
By the ringing Harlequin.

And in the corner, beneath the icons,
In the swirling multicolored crowd,
Spinning his childish eyes,
The deceived Pierrot trembles.
(*7 October 1902*)

153

Freedom gazes into the blueness.
The window is open. The air is sharp.
A section of the moon hides
Behind yellow-red foliage.

At night it will be a bright sickle,
Sparkling on night's harvest.
Its setting, its waning
Caresses the eyes for the last time.

As then, the window rings
But my voice, like the fresh air,
Sang its song long ago and grew silent
Under the reeds at the shore.

How pale the moon is in the blueness,
How golden the fine hair…
How forgotten, withered, and dead
Is the ear of grain swaying in the foliage…
(*10 October 1902*)

 154

He went away and hid in the night,
No one knows where.
On his desk he left his keys
And inside the desk, an indication of a trace.

Did anyone think then
That he would not return home?
The nighttime riding had abated—
He was betrothed to the Woman.

On the white cold snow
He had killed his heart.

Meantime he thought he was walking with Her
In the meadow amid white lilies.

The morning light is glimmering
But he is still not home.
His fiancée is waiting for him in vain.
He had been there, but he will not return.
(*12 October 1902*)

*Religio*

1.

I loved tender words.
I sought mysterious racemes.
And having barely recovered my vision,
I was uproarious, like children at their games.

But going out into the meadow in the early morning
And humming obscure tunes,
I knew You, my eternal friend,
You, my Protectress Virgin.

I, a pensive poet, knew
That not a single genius had known
Such freedom as the vow
Of my Ministries as a slave.
(*18 October 1902*)

2.

A silent phantom in a tower,
I am a low slave of accursed blood.
I observe half-darkness
In Her untouched alcove.

I guard Her keys
And am present with Her, unseen,
When swords clash for the beauty
Of Her who is Unattainable.

My voice is hollow, my hair is gray.
My face twitches horribly.
My life is governed by one Testament:
The Testament of service of Her who is Unfathomable.
(*18 October 1902*)

 156

I enter dark temples
And celebrate a poor rite.
I await there the Beautiful Lady
In the glow of red lamps.

In shadow by a tall column
I tremble from the creak of the doors,
While into my face gazes, illumined,
Only Her image, only the dream of Her.

O, I have grown accustomed to these vestments
Of the majestic Eternal Woman!
High above in the cornices
Flash smiles, fairy tales, and dreams.

O Holy One, how tender are the candles,
How comforting Your features!
I hear neither sighs nor words
But I believe: You are the Dear one.
(*25 October 1902*)

 157

You are holy, but I do not believe You.
I long know everything beforehand:
The day will come when the doors will open
And a white procession will pass by.

Frightening and indescribable will be
The unearthly masks of the faces…
Crazy and outstretched on the ground,
I will call to You: "Hosanna!"

And then, rising above all things that perish,
You will reveal Your Radiant Face.
And, free of earthly captivity,
I will pour my whole life into a final shout.
(*29 October 1902*)

 158

A day will come that will be like an instant of gaiety
When we will forget all names.
You yourself will come into my cell
And awaken me from my dream.

From my face, seized with trembling,
You will guess my thoughts.
But the whole past will become a lie
As soon as Your Rays start shining.

As then, with a silent smile
You will read on my brow
About shaky and faithless love,
About love that blossomed on earth.

But then—more majestically and beautifully
And without doubts and thoughts
I, partaking of Your Day,
Will receive and drink to the bottom the cup.
(*31 October 1902*)

159

He was encountered everywhere
In the streets on sleepy days.
He'd walk and carry his miracle,
Stumbling in the frosty shadows.

He'd enter his quiet cell,
Light the last light,
And place on the table a lamp for gaiety
And a sumptuous bouquet of lilies.

People, laughing, would marvel at him
And call him a queer fellow.
He'd think about a fur jacket
And again disappear in the dusk.

Once they walked him home—
He was gay and happy;
But in the morning they put him in the grave
And the priest officiated quietly.
(*October 1902*)

 160

Mysterious signs flare up
On the hopelessly blind wall.
Gold and red poppies
Hang over me in my sleep.

I hide in nocturnal caves
And do not remember the severe miracles.
At dawn blue chimeras
Look out from the mirror of the bright heavens.

I flee into past instants
And close my eyes in fear;
On the pages of the cold book
Is a maiden's golden braid.[20]

Above me the firmament is already low,
A black dream weighs on my breast.
My predestined end is near;
Both war and fire are ahead.
(*October 1902*)

❦161❦

I am afraid to meet You
But I am more afraid not to meet You.
I am amazed by everything;
On everything I detect the mark.

Shadows move in the street;
I do not know if they're alive or asleep.
Clinging to the church steps,
I am afraid to look back.

They lay their hands on my shoulders
But I do not remember their names.
In my ears reverberate the sounds
Of recent large funerals.

The somber sky hangs low—
It has even covered the temple.
I know: You are here. You are near.
You are not here. You are—there.
(*5 November 1902*)

---

20  The Russian word for braid (kosa) can also mean scythe.

162

Homes grow like desires,
But if suddenly you were to look back,
There where the white building used to be,
You'd see black filth.

Thus all things are displaced,
Imperceptibly rise upward.
You, Orpheus, lost your bride—
Who whispered to you: "Look back"?

I will cover my head with white,
Scream, and throw myself into the stream.
And a fragrant flower of the river
Will float up and sway over my body.
(*5 November 1902*)

# Crossroads[1]

(1902–1904)

PETERSBURG—Bad Nauheim—Shakhmatovo

I guarded them in the chapel of John;
A motionless guard, I guarded the light of the lamps.

And here She is, and to Her is my Hosanna—
The crown of works is higher than all rewards.

I hid my face and the years passed.
I performed my Service for many years.

The vaults were illumined with evening rays
And she gave me Her Royal Answer.[2]

Here I alone guarded and lit the candles.
Alone—a prophet—I trembled in the censers' smoke.

And on That Day—the sole participant of the Meeting—
I did not share those Meetings with anyone.
(*8 November 1902*)

I stand in power, lonely in soul,
Ruler of earthly beauty.
You, night flower full of passion,
Fell in love with my features.
Bending low to my breast,

---

1 Plural in the Russian.
2 Liubov Dmitrievna Mendeleeva had accepted Blok's proposal of marriage on 7 November 1902.

You are sad, my spring flower.
Here the heart is near, but up ahead
There is no unriddling for life.

And all-powerful, I calculate as in the past;
I conjure and divine again
How with passionate life I, a wise king,
Can combine You, Love?[3]
(*14 November 1902*)

       3
*I dream of the impossible again.*
Fet[4]

The pale sunset lingers in the sky,
A cock crows in the distance.
On the fields in the ripening grain
A little worm glows and goes out.

The alder branches grow dark,
A light is twinkling beyond the river.
Through the rarefied magical mist
An invisible herd of horses has galloped.

I ride through the sorrowful fields,
Humming a sorrowful tune.
Impossible dreams disappear
Behind my shoulders, having possessed my soul.

I whisper and compose verses—
There is something fantastic in my thoughts.
And the gray boughs sway
As if they have arms and faces.
(*17 November 1902*)

3  In Russian the name of his betrothed (Liubov') means "Love."
4  From Fet's poem "It is still spring…"

I've put on multicolored feathers,
Hardened my wings—and wait.
Above me and beneath me is mistrust;
The darkness disperses—I wait.

Submerged in slumber, here sit
Birds, my companions of former years.
They have forgotten everything, do not believe in flight,
And do not see what I am capable of.

These pale sleepy birds
Will not fly up in a flock in the morning;
They will not notice the twinkling of the morning star;
They will not understand the exclamation: "It's time!"

 But my white wings will flash,
And they will fold and close,
Burdened by dreams of powerlessness
And falling asleep for long days.
(*21 November 1902*)

*Song of Ophelia*

Yesterday he whispered much to me,
He whispered things that are terrifying, terrifying...
He departed by a sorrowful road,
    And I forgot yesterday—
        forgot yesterday.

This was yesterday—is it long ago?
Why is he so silent?
I did not find my lilies in the field.
    I did not seek the weeping willow—
        the weeping willow.

Oh, is that long ago! To me, to me
He spoke—and kissed me...
And I do not remember, do not remember
    What the shores were whispering—
        the shores were whispering.

I saw in every blade of grass
His dear terrifying face...
He departed by that same path
    On which yesterday departed—
        yesterday departed.

I found refuge in the field alone
And my sorrow disappeared.
This was yesterday—is it long ago?
    To me he spoke and kissed me—
        kissed me.
(*23 November 1902*)

 6

Weary and wise, having
Risen from a troubled sleep,
I lower to the ground my banners
Before You, Golden-haired Maiden.

It is the end of my omniscient pride—
Having fallen out of love with the former darkness
And devoted to Holiness forever,
I will obey You in all things.

The winter will pass—in the singing blizzard
There is already a distant ringing.
The royal arcs have closed,
My soul is blissful, You are near.
(*30 November 1902*)

*The Voice*

The winter mists are hot—
The heavenly vault is all in blood.
I am going to the foreign lands
Of sacramentalized love.

You are in my dreams. I do not gift you
With my embraces at night.
I am the empress of stellar hosts;
My rays are not for you.

You are deceived by the unknown:
For holy dreams
It is impossible for incorporeal beings
To reveal their features.

Bury yourself even more passionlessly
In the darkness of your spirit:
You will understand that I am more beautiful
Than your apparition.
(*3 December 1902*)

I will guard my torch
At the entrance to the sultry garden.
You will weave flower and leaf
High above along the fence.

A flower—a star in tears of dew—
Will run down to me from the heights.
I will be the guard of its beauty—
A silent astronomer.

But in the passionate hour the wall is low;
The forbidden flower is loved.

Following the track of the first flower,
You will show the way for others.

The flowery stream will flow—
And the stars are numberless.
And I will lose strict count
Of flowers entrained by the stream.
(*4 December 1902*)

We are everywhere. We are nowhere. We walk
And the winter wind blows at us.
In churches both at dusk and during the day
It sings and blows out the candles.

And it often seems that in the distance,
At dark walls or at a corner
Where we sang and passed,
There still sings and walks Someone.

I gaze at the winter wind:
I am afraid to understand and go into it.
I grow pale. I wait. But I will not say
For whom it is time to stir.

I know everything. But we two are together.
There can be no question now
That we are not walking here alone,
That Someone is blowing out the candles.
(*5 December 1902*)

### 10
*To Andrey Bely*

I gazed at the blind structure for habitation;
Under the roof a window was slowly being lit up.
Someone above heard my approach
And thought about what had been long ago.

The curtains stirred and fell.
They were raised by an invisible hand.
On the stairs shadows were swaying.
And cautious bells started ringing.

No one had yet started climbing the stairs
But the counting of the steps could already be heard.
And everywhere they were waking up, shouting, watching out
for the messenger,
And gray heads were bending down into the shadows.

They thought: the morning would be followed by day.

Above all the tousled shouters,
Under the roof a window was slowly being lit up.
There someone had counted on a gilded abacus
What no one is given to count.

I understood that it would be dark.
(*5 December 1902*)


### 11

The tsaritsa[5] was looking at the book's headpieces—
Red-gilded letters.
She lit red icon-lamps
And prayed to the meek Theotokos.

---

5  Wife of a tsar, or empress.

The tsaritsa passed her blue nights
Over the Deep book.[6]
Meantime to the Tsarevna[7] white birds
Would fly down from the dove tower.

The Tsarevna scattered grains
And the white feathers quivered.
The doves cooed obediently
In the tower—beneath the decoratively carved door.

The Tsarevna is more rosy-cheeked than the tsaritsa,
Than the tsaritsa who seeks meaning.
Every page of the book has
Gold and red numbers.

A high cloud burst open
And the Dove book fell.
A cooing bird flew to the Tsarevna
From the azure eye.

It is so languid and sweet for the Tsarevna –
The Tsarevna-Bride is like an icon-lamp.
The tsaritsa has blue riddles—
Gold and red headpieces.

Bow down, tsaritsa, to the Tsarevna,
To the golden-haired Tsarevna:
From your ancient deepness—
From your wise dove meekness.

6  The "Deep" (Glubinnaya) or "Dove" (Golubinnaya) book is a famous work of
old Russian religious literature—"Deep" because of its spiritual profundity, "Dove"
because it is permeated by the Holy Spirit.
7  Daughter of a tsar.

You are strong, tsaritsa, by your deepness;
Your book has gilded pages.

Meantime the Bride with her innocence alone
Will outpray your numbers, tsaritsa.
(*14 December 1902*)

 12

Here she[8] is—in the in-rushing wave
She burned with ultimate revenge;
In the reeds she ran across the bottom
As smoldering red tidings.

But in vain is her alluring attire;
Admire, instead, her shining armor:
On the stern motionlessly stand
Men with breasts pointed toward the sunset.

You do not see calm strongholds,
We are not afraid of your tempests.
Throw the smoldering torch
Into untroubled blue waters.
(*24 December 1902*)

 13

They were all shouting at round tables
And restlessly changing places.
There was a fog from alcohol fumes.
Suddenly someone entered—and through the roar of the voices
He said: "This is my bride."

8 Allusion to "Maiden-Offense" in *The Song of Igor's Campaign.*

[144]

No one heard anything.
They were all squealing furiously like beasts.
And one of them, having no idea why,

Was swaying and laughing, pointing at him
And at the girl who had entered the room.

She dropped her handkerchief
And each of them, with spiteful energy,
As if having understood the sinister hint,
Tore from it a shred with a squeal
And colored it with blood and dust.

After they had all gone back to the table,
Grew quiet, and sat down in their places,
He pointed out to them the girl in the corner
And said distinctly, piercing the darkness:
"Gentlemen! This is my bride!"

And suddenly the one who had been swaying and laughing,
Absurdly extending his arms,
Now hugged the table and shuddered,
And those who had been shouting insanely,
Now heard sounds of weeping.
(*25 December 1902*)

 14

The steps were growing red and fading.
You had said: "I will come."
At the entrance to the darkness of prayers
I opened my heart.—I wait.

What I will say to you—I do not know.
Perhaps I will die of happiness.
But burning with the evening fire,
I will draw you too to the bonfire.

The red flame blossoms.
Unexpectedly the dreams were fulfilled.
You are coming. Above the temple, above us—
There is sunsetless depth and height.
(*25 December 1902*)

 15

I sought the blue road
And shouted, deafened by people;
Approaching the golden threshold,
I grew quiet before Your doors.

You passed into distant halls,
Majestic, quiet, and severe.
I carried Your shawl after You
And gazed at Your pearls.
(*December 1902*)

 16

We withdrew—and strained to raise
The gay flag into the night skies
As, down below, incoherent human
Voices fought and shouted.

And here is the dawn of final consciousness—
They shout in unprecedented battle,
The tested building shakes,
But around me is the airy dream in You.
(*December 1902*)

 17

She waited and thrashed in death agony.
Already beckoning, like a call from afar,

Dark hands were stretched toward her
And her own uncertain hand was drawn toward them.

Suddenly a gust of sleepy spring wind blew in
And snuffed out the candle; it grew quiet
And an imposing voice, a benevolent voice,
Sang upstairs like a fine string.
(*December 1902*)

 18

Singing dream, blossoming flower,
Disappearing day, fading light.

Opening the window, I saw lilac.
This was in the spring—on a day that flew by.

The flowers breathed freely—and the shadows of joyful
Garments shifted onto the dark cornice.

The anguish was waning, the soul was on fire;
I opened the window, shaking and trembling.

And I do not remember but it is as if she breathed into my face,
And, singing and burning, she ascended the steps of the porch.
(*September–December 1902*)

 19
*To Andrey Bely*

The whole year the window hadn't shaken,
The heavy door hadn't rattled;
All was forgotten—forgotten long ago,
And it opened now.

They were fussing and hastily crossing themselves...
They were carrying out a silver coffin...

[147]

And an old woman, holding on to the handle,
Was stumbling over a snowbank.

The indifferent faces of the crowd,
An inflow of curious neighbors...
All around they had made paths with their feet,
Profaning the chaste snow.

But lying down in the bed of snow,
The one confined in the coffin
Heard the blizzard singing in the distance,
Lifting its horn to the sky.
(*6 January 1902*)

 20

Here the night is dead. My words are strange.
A red phantom glimmers—the dawn.
In the morning into the heavens I will launch my shouts
Like white birds to meet the Emperor.

In dream and in waking reality—indistinguishable are
Dawn and fire glow, stillness and fear...
My insanities are my cherubim....
My Terrifying one, my Near one is the black monk...

Is it a hand or the wind that stirs the rags?
The bony fingers are shreds of grasses...
Green eyes burn at the crossroads—
There the wind makes an empty sleeve flap...

Is one face closed or are many closed?
Do you know? You see! The clothes are empty!...
Before morning—without the sun—I will launch my shouts
Like black birds to meet Christ!
(*9 January 1903*)

21

I will not go out to meet people—
I will be afraid of their censure and their praise.
Only before You will I answer
For having been silent my whole life.

I understand silent people
And I like those who have turned into hearing:
Behind the words, through an incoherent din,
A radiant Spirit is awakened.

I will go out into a holiday of silence;
People will not notice my face.
But in me is hidden knowledge
Of love for You without end.
(*14 January 1903*)

 22

In epistles to earthly rulers
I spoke of Eternal Hope.
They did not believe my cries
And I am not the same as before.

I will not reveal to anyone now
What is begotten in my thought.
Let them think I am in the wilderness,
Wandering, languishing, and calculating.

But, God! What epistles
I am sending now to the One Most Pure.
My fateful knowledge
Has penetrated deep into the radiant darkness...

And only one woman in the world
Is reflected in each syllable...

But she is a participant in the feast
In your—O God!—palace.
(*27 January 1903*)

 23

Here the memory of the holy wave
Remains like a foamy trace.
Sorrowless, I follow You—
My unknown path is known to me.

When and where you will lead me,
I do not know but there is no doubt
That the former lie has perished
And the whirlwind of visions is at hand.

When my hour comes
And my favorite songs cease,
Here they will sorrowfully say: "He was snuffed out."
But There one will hear: "Rise from the dead!"
(*31 January 1903*)

 24

The halls have darkened and faded;
The window lattice has grown black.
The vassals were whispering at the doors:
"The queen, the queen is sick."

And the king, furrowing his brow,
Would walk by without pages and servants.
And every word he let drop
Hinted at the deathly ailment.

At the doors of the hushed bedroom
I was weeping, squeezing the ring.

There—at the end of the far gallery—
Someone, his face covered, echoed me.

At the doors of the Incomparable Lady
I was sobbing in my sky-blue cloak.
And, unsteady on his feet, the same stranger
With a pale face echoed me.
(*4 February 1903*)

 25

The old woman was conjuring at the entrance
About things that had happened long ago.
And suddenly above the crowd of people
A window opened with a ringing sound.
Card after card rustled.
The dark door grew black.
And people, filled with excitement,
Wanted to know—what now?
No one had heard the ringing sound—
Some chatterer had been talking.
But up there, in the balcony grating,
The pig iron was shaking and singing.
Up there, the dark beams had cracked
And the glass in the window had shattered.
And suddenly the conjurer's face
Started shining—it became bright with light.
But those who learned of the magic belatedly
And saw the terrible face—
They were choking in the smoke of the fire
And emitting piercing screams.
Above the ruins of the collapsed buildings
A red worm was wriggling.
In the deserted place of the conjuration
Someone rose—and unfurled a flag.
(*13 February 1903*)

I sank into a sea of clover,
Surrounded by the fairy-tales of bees.
But the wind, calling from the north,
Found my childlike heart.

It was calling to a battle of the plains—
For a struggle with the breathing of the sky.
It showed me a desolate road,
Disappearing in dark woods.

I follow it over sloping ground,
Looking ceaselessly ahead.
In front with innocent gazes
Advances my childlike heart.

My sleepless eyes may become weary,
The dust may sing and grow red,
But the flowers and bees that are in love—
They told not a fairy tale, but what is real.
(*18 February 1903*)

The winter wind plays with the blackthorn
And blows out the candle in the window.
You have left for a rendezvous with your lover.
I am alone. I will forgive. I am silent.

You do not know to whom you are praying—
He is playing and joking with you.
You will be pricked by the cold blackthorn,
Returning home at night.

But having long listened to happiness,
I will wait for you at the window.

You surrender yourself to him with passion.
It doesn't matter. I keep your secret.

All that has grown murky in your heart
Will become clear in my stillness.
And when you and he part,
You will confess only to me.
(*20 February 1903*)

Again I walk above this desolate plain.
My heart is powerless to find shelter in obscure doubts.
That which I came to love in your swanlike beauty,
Is eternally beautiful, but my heart is unhappy.

I do not conceal that I weep when I worship you
But, having gone beyond human language,
I am silent and smile at you in my tears:
The leave-takings of the heart—and new meetings.

The sky has turned dark again and there will be storms.
A heart in love can find no shelter from pain.
In the same way, a happy man is afraid his happiness will end
And a free man is afraid of captivity.
(*22 February 1903*)

"Are the people calm?"
"No. The Emperor has been killed.
Someone is preaching
A new freedom in the squares."

"Is everyone ready to rise up?"
"No. They're waiting with stony fixity.
Someone has ordered them to wait:
They're roaming about and singing songs."

"Who has been placed in power?"
"The people don't want power.
Civic passions slumber:
It is rumored that someone is coming."

"Who is he? A tamer of the people?"
"He is dark, cruel, and ferocious:
A monk saw him at the monastery entrance
And turned blind.

To unplumbed abysses
He chases men like herds...
 He chases them with an iron staff..."[9]
"O God! Let us flee from the Judgment!"
(*3 March 1903*)

The work is finished.
The days are numbered.
We prayed here
By the sleepy river.

Over there the ice floes rushed past
In the days of spring.
And the days have been forgotten!
How distant they are!

My finished day
Ended itself.

9  Cf. Revelation 2:27.

My naked spirit
Sings for everyone.
Weary and in love,
I wait for you,
I who am sullen, sleepless,
And as cold as ice.
(*4 March 1903*)

 31

I dreamt cheerful thoughts,
I dreamt I am not alone…
Just before morning I awoke from the noise
And roar of ice floes rushing by.

I thought of the realized miracle…
Over there, having sharpened their axes,
Red cheerful men,
Laughing, were building bonfires.

They tarred the heavy boats…
The river, singing, carried
Blue ice floes, waves,
And a splinter of an oar…

Drunk with the cheerful noise,
My soul was full of unheard-of things…
With me is my springtime thought:
I know You are not alone…
(*11 March 1903*)

 32

Doors are opening—there's a glimmering;
And outside the bright window there are visions.
I do not know, and will not hide that I do not know;
But I will fall asleep—and dreams will come.

In the still air there is some hiding and knowing thing...
Something is hidden and laughing there.
What is laughing? Is it my sighing
Heart that is so joyously beating?

Is it the spring outside the windows—rosy, sleepy?
Or is it the Bright Maiden smiling at me?
Or is it only my heart in love?
Or does it all only seem? Or is it all recognized?
(*17 March 1903*)

 33

I carved a staff out of oak
Under the blizzard's caressing whispers.
My clothes are poor and rough;
Oh, how unworthy are my female friends!

But, even paupered, I will find the road;
Come out, frosty sun!
I will roam all day taking what God gives me
And in the evening I will knock on the window...

And a secret door will be opened
For me by the white hand
Of a young maiden with a golden braid
And a clear, open soul.

The moon and the stars are in her braid...
"Enter, my pleasing prince..."
And my poor oak staff
Will glitter with a semiprecious tear...
(*25 March 1903*)

❧ 34 ❧

*To S. Solovyov*

Grass sprouted at the forgotten graves.
We forgot yesterday… And we forgot all words…
   And all around it grew quiet…

By this death of those who have departed and disappeared,
Are You not alive? Are You not full of light?
   Is Your heart not spring?

This is the only place I can breathe, at the foot of these graves,
Where I once had composed gentle songs
   About a possible meeting with You…

Where for the first time You breathed
Into my waxlike features like a breeze of distant life,
   Sprouting up as the grass at the grave.
(*1 April 1903*)

❧ 35 ❧

*A.M. Dobroliubov*[10]
A.M.D. with his blood
He had scrawled on the shield.
Pushkin[11]

Out of the fog of the city,
Drawing with his stick on the ground,
Coldly, strangely, and early,
Departed the sick child.
As if playing blind man's buff
With Eternity, the sick boy,

10  Alexander Mikhailovich Dobroliubov (1876–1944), a famous figure of the Silver
Age. He started as a decadent poet in the 1890s, but abandoned literature to become a
mysterious religious wanderer and teacher.

11  From Pushkin's poem "Legend," about a knight's faithfulness. A.M.D. (coincid-
ing with Dobroliubov's initials) stands for "Ave Mater Dei" ("Hail Mother of God").

On his pilgrimage, draws figures
And challenges to battle.
His voice is bold and high-pitched,
His project is childishly sublime.
The weak and frail child
Carries a little stalk in his hand.
This stalk of the universal work
He caresses, calling out: "Pray!"
The feeble body became
Entwined with stalks of flowers...
They rise higher
And will soon ascend to the sky...
His voice grows quieter and quieter...
He will soon weep—and understand.
(*10 April 1903*)

 36

At a small grave on a green shore
On Annunciation Day they were singing a psalm.
White priests were burying with a smile
A little girl in a sky-blue dress.

All of them—with the help of the Higher Will—
Blossomed in the blood of God the Heavenly Father
And gently offered incense to heaven,
Not from the censer but seemingly from the green earth itself.
(*24 April 1903*)

 37

I was dressed in multicolored rags,
White and red, and wore a grotesque mask.
I laughed and made a fool of myself at crossroads
And told funny fairy-tales.
I unfolded long narratives—
Incoherently, endlessly, juicily—

About old men, about lands without name,
About a girl with infant's eyes.

Some laughed long and senselessly;
Others were pained.
And when I'd suddenly lose the thread,
The crowd would yell: "Enough!"
(*April 1903*)

 38

A black figure ran around the city.
Scrambling up a staircase, he put out the little lamps.

Slow and white, the sunrise approached,
And climbed up the staircase with the figure.

Over there, in a place of soft, gentle shadows—
One saw yellow bands of evening lamps—

The morning twilight spread over the steps
And crept into the curtains and the cracks in the doors.

Ah, how pale the city is at dawn!
The little black figure is weeping in the yard.
(*April 1903*)

 39

I wake up and in the field it is misty,
But from my tower I can point to the sun.
My awakening is beyond desire,
Like the girl whom I serve.

When at dusk I was passing by on the road,
I noticed a little red light in the window.

A rosy girl came out to the doorway
And told me I am handsome and tall.

That's my whole fairy tale, good people.
I need nothing else from you:
I never dreamt of a miracle,
And you should calm down—and forget about him.
(*2 May 1903*)

You wore a closed black dress.
You never lifted Your eyes.
Only on your breast, perhaps, above the cross,
The gauze stirred and sometimes rose.

Your voice was silvery-weary.
Your speech was mysteriously simple.
Someone Strong and Knowing, perhaps In Love
With His Creation, had locked Your lips.

Who He was, I do not know and will never know,
But I am jealous of Him and fearful of Him.
I am jealous of the Deity to Whom I compose songs,
But the songs I compose are dedicated to I do not know Whom.
(*15 May 1903, Petersburg*)

When I was becoming old and decrepit,
A poet accustomed to his gray hair,
I got the urge to push back
The end destined for all old men.
And I, ill and feeble,
Seek again the happy star.

An image formerly dear
Appears to me in my aged delirium.
Perhaps my memory has betrayed me
But I do not believe in this lie,
And nothing has been awakened
By this captivating shiver.
All those fables are far away now—
They captivated me in my young years,
But old age has bent my shoulders
And it amuses me that I am a poet…
I am tired of believing the pitiful books
Of such rosy idiots as I was!
Accursed be dreams! Accursed be the instants
Of my prophetic verses!
Alone with myself,
I become decrepit, dry up, am choked by spite,
And with wrinkled hand
I strain to lift my cane…
Whom can I believe? With whom can I make peace?
Physicians, poets, and priests…
O, if I could only learn
The immortal vulgarity of the rabble!
(*4 June 1903, Bad Nauheim*)

A fiddle moans at the foot of the mountain.
In the sleepy park the evening is long,
The evening is long—and the Innocent Image,
The Image of the girl, is with me.

The fiddle's tireless moan
Sings to me: "Live…"
The image of the beloved girl
Is a tale of tender love.
(*June 1903, Bad Nauheim*)

She was fifteen. But judging by the beating
Of my heart, she could have been my bride.
When I, laughing, offered her my hand,
She laughed and left.

That was long ago. Since then
Many obscure days and years have passed.
We met rarely and spoke little
But our silences were deep.

One winter night, true to a dream I had,
I fled certain crowded brightly lit halls
Where stifling masks were smiling at the singing
And where my eyes had been greedily following her.

She followed me out, submissive,
Having no idea of what was to come.
Only the black city night saw
How bride and bridegroom went out and hid.

And on a frosty sunny red day
We met in the temple—in deep quiet:
We understood that the years of silence were clear
And what had happened, had happened in the heights.
This story of long blissful seekings
Fills my sultry singing breast.
From these songs I have erected a building;
As for the other songs, I will sing them some other time.
(*16 June 1903, Bad Nauheim*)

The day was gently gray, melancholy gray.
The evening became pearly white, like a woman's hand.
In the evening rooms they hid their hearts,
Weary of the endless gentle melancholy.

They pressed hands, avoided meetings,
Concealed their laughter by the whiteness of their shoulders.

They bent over the tablecloths in the dining rooms,
Touching their burning faces with their coiffures.

The heart beat faster, the gaze became more intense;
He was in her thoughts—a deep tender sultry garden.

And silently, as if by a sign, they went downstairs.
On the steps a woman's white garments rustled.

Silently, they sank in the garden without a trace.
The sky quietly burst forth with a fire of shame.

Perhaps a red star had rolled down.
(June 1903. Bad Nauheim)

 45

The dock is silent. The land is near.
The land is invisible. The night is deep.

I am standing on gray wet boards.
The storm is laughing into my gray curls.

I seem to hear, to hear my own shout:
"Place a candle on a rock in the sea!

When my wife's boat docks,
She and I will both be saved!"

I am afraid, and the waves beat hard
Against the wet sand, sending their hoary hint…
She is far away. There is no answer.
Accursed sea, give me an answer!

There is a rock in the distance! Place a candle there!
I do not know if I am the one shouting.
(*July 1903, Shakhmatovo*)

 46

I am a double-edged sword.
An archangel, I rule Her Fate.
A green stone burns in my shield.
It was lit not by me, but by the Lord's hand.

I will offer him my immeasurableness
When I depart into eternal sleep.
To Her in the world I will leave my candle,
My stone, and the sound of my earthly ringing.

As Her guard I will place my ringing verse.
The green stone I will light in Her heart.
And the stone will be Her friend and bridegroom,
And it will not lie to Her, just as I do not lie.
(*July 1903*)

 47
*The Double*

Here is my song to you, Columbine.
It bears the stamp of gloomy constellations:
Only in the costume of the clown Harlequin
Am I able to compose such songs.

There are two of us—we are trudging through the marketplace;
Both of us are wearing clown costumes with bells.
Hey, come admire this dumb pair
And listen to the ringing of the jaunty bells!
People walk by, saying: "You, passerby,
Are exactly like me and like everyone else,

But behind you walks a hunchbacked beggar
With satchel and crutch who doesn't resemble you at all."

What passerby would find us worthy of a glance?
Who could guess that we two are together?
The decrepit old man repeats to me: "Soon."
I repeat: "Let us go, let us go."

If a passerby looks at us indifferently,
He smiles, I tremble.
I shout spitefully: "I'm bored! I'm hot!"
He repeats: "Walk on. I won't let you go."

There, where into the street, into the ringing throng,
A rosy countenance peers and hides,
We enter a crowded shop:
I—Harlequin and, behind me, the old man.

O, if only they could notice, notice,
And look into my eyes behind the multicolored costume!
Perhaps next to me they would encounter
My own sly laughing gaze!

Over there is Columbine's blue window,
The rosy evening, the sleeping window ledge…
In a merriment of death we two Harlequins—
Young and old—embrace and are intertwined!…

O, separate us! You can see:
We have the same eyes, though our costumes are different!…
The old man stupidly mocks you;
The young man is a brother tenderly devoted to you!

She who is at the window is rosier than the evenings;
She who is above is more dazzling than the day!
It is Columbine! O men! O beasts!
Be like children. Understand me.
(*30 July 1903, Shakhmatovo*)

### ❧ 48 ❧

Above this autumn you have roared like a storm
Through all things and grown weary.
But I stand near with my sword,
Having lowered for a time my visor.

Tame your soul's seething rage
As I will my accursed bravery.
What remain are the dawn's red call
And fidelity to the blue banner.

We are on the true path
And have evaded captivity not for the first time.
Lead me. In order to go through everything,
We need unearthly powers.
(*22 August 1903, Shakhmatovo*)

### ❧ 49 ❧
*Pussy-Willow Saturday*[12]

The evening people return to their homes.
A blue night is lit over the city.
Princesses quietly return to their towers.
Spring gusts and cavorts on the street.

On the street is a holiday, on the street is light,
And candles and pussy willows greet the dawn.
Incoherent delirious slumber—
The tsar dreams of foreign guests...
The princes dream of...—"Wake up, we are here..."
The princess is drooping sleepily in the darkness...
Over there, shadows move and visions float...
That which was in heaven is now on earth...

---

12 Celebrated in Russia eight days before Easter. In western Christianity it corresponds to the day before Palm Sunday.

Spring morning. Pensive sleep.
Guests in love, guests from foreign clans
And perhaps of late, merry times.

Transparent cloud. Pearly pattern.
There was a rendezvous there. There was a conversation there...

And just before morning my soul was opened
By a pale hand and lit by the rosy dawn.
(*2 September 1903, Petersburg*)

My moon is in royal zenith.
I will bathe in nocturnal freedom
And there—I will wrap myself in silver threads
In an excess of happiness.

Going to meet the passionate captivity
And the coming Dawn,
I nod to the blue expanses
And plunge into the dark silver!...

In the squares of the steamy capital,
Blind people say:
"What is above the earth? An air balloon.
What is under the moon? A blimp."

As for me, I speed through a silver desert
In feverish delirium.
And in the folds of my dark-blue vestment
I have hidden my Beloved Star.
(*1 October 1903*)

### ❦❦51❦❦

She returned in the dead of night. Till dawn
She kept going up to the blue windows of the sitting room.
Where had she been? She left and didn't say.
   Could it be my turn?

In agitation I roam about the sitting room...
In these windows there is a hint.
All night these doors threw at me
Creaks, shadows, perhaps a reproach?...

Tomorrow I will go into my quarters
When she comes to me to sob.
I will lower the white blinds
And curtain off my bed.

Timid, I will lie down, smiling at the moment,
And all alone, having bitten into the final bread,
I will become immersed in the mysterious book
   Of fulfilled destinies.
(*9 October 1903*)

### ❦❦52❦❦
*To Andrey Bely*

   I ran and stumbled,
   Bled profusely, smashed
   Against cliffs, rose to my feet,
   And kept praying as I continued to run.
   Suddenly there was a cold breeze.
   In front of me I saw the reddening dawn.
   Someone with a ringing, summoning sledge-hammer
   Was putting up the pillars of a sanctuary.
   At the frightening line of the horizon,
   Where the earth abruptly ended,
   I imagined I saw you dying,

Bleeding profusely like me.
   Can it be that you too are retreating?
   Can it be that I am now alone?
   Or are you testing me by waving
   A bloody cloth in the field?
O, I have seen it, unhappy man that I am,
I have seen the red cloth of the fields…
Is it the dawn unleashing its red war-cry?
Is it the thought of Her bursting forth in me?
   It is the dawn of infinite cold,
   Sending me its sweet hint,
   Scattering its red gold,
   Spreading the bloody cloth.
Your soul is forged by fire
And devoted to the universal dream.
It is excited by the impossible dream
Of guessing Her Names.
(*18 October 1903*)

# 53 #

*Immanuel Kant*

I am sitting behind a screen.[13] I have
Such tiny feet,
Such little hands,
Such a dark little window…
It is warm and dark. I put out
The candle they bring in,
But I offer gratitude…
They've long been asking me to divert myself,

---

13  This image is taken from Andrey Bely's *Dramatic Symphony*, where a young philosopher, who after reading in Kant's *Critique of Pure Reason* that space and time are a priori forms of knowledge, wonders if it is possible to hide from space and time by putting screens around oneself.

But these little hands... I am in love
With my wrinkled skin...
I could have a sweet dream
But I will not trouble myself:
I will not trouble forgetfulness,
These sun specks on the little window...
And I cross my little hands
And I also cross my little feet.
I am sitting behind a screen. It is warm here.
There is someone here. There is no need for a candle.
My eyes are bottomless like glass.
On my wrinkled hand are little rings.
(*18 October 1903*)

 54

...And I approach the window again,
In love with the shimmering saga.
I don't listen long to the quiet:
Exhausted, I lie down again.

I have left the day to take my repose,
And I chase away sleep to prolong the silence...
In the daytime nobody feels sorry for me—
At night I feel sorry for my suffering...
In the sleepless silence
It pours out solemn torments for me.
And someone dear and near to me
Squeezes my sorrowing hands...
(*26 October 1903*)

 55

When I withdraw to my repose from the times,
When I withdraw from censure and praise,
You should remember that tenderness, that caressing dream,
By which I blossomed and breathed.

I know, Radiant One,[14] You will not remember the evil
That was thrashing in me
When You came up, statuesquely white
Like a swan, to my depths,

It was not I who disturbed Your proud laziness;
It was an alien power.
A cold cloud agitated my day—
Your day was more radiant than mine.

You will remember—when I withdraw to my repose,
When I disappear beyond the blue horizon—
A certain song which I sang with You
And which You repeated after me.
(*1 November 1903*)

### 56
#### To Andrey Bely

Yes. I knew. And you blew out
   The bright torch, pining away
      In the smoky dusk.
In the abyss there's darkness while in heaven there's din.
   Dear friend! Another star
      Has been revealed to us on earth.

Inseparably—we two together
Will bear a vow to Eternity.
We will meet late at the grave
On the silver path.

There—I will press the gentle hand
Of the one pressing hands.
I will firmly embrace
The one silent with torment.

14  In the Russian this is feminine.

Yes. I heard the news of the new thing!
The mask of the mourning soul!
On That Day—with a familiar word
You will again stun my heart!

And then—in the thunderous sphere
Of unprecedented fire—
The radiant sword will open for us the doors
Of the Dazzling Day.
(*1 November 1903*)

At the fireplace, with your gray head bent,
You are listening to fairy tales in verse.
Behind you, we—invisible dreams—
Are drawing a pattern on the walls.

Your daughter—in the armchair—is rosier than the spring
And more severe than the evening shadows.
In her presence we never knocked
Or did any mischief.

How radiant and good it is in your room—
Behind the wall we find it dark...
Let us do mischief, let us knock on the glass,
Let us even hide in the window!

Gently raising your gray head, you will say:
"Did you hear a knocking somewhere, my friend?"
Your daughter, who is rosier than the spring,
Will say: "It's some little gray animal."
(*1 November 1903*)

58

Her porch is like a parvis.
I enter—and the storm abates.
There's a patterned cloth on the table
And icons hidden in the corner.

Her face is colored with a gentle rosiness,
The stillness of illumined shadows.
In my soul is a swirling dance
Of my days that have flown away.

It has been long since I encountered this rosiness
And my dawn is murkily still.
And in every swirl of the dance
I see a flame of sin.

Such quiet joy is gifted
Only to final intoxications.
I came to her with bitter merriment
To drink my cup to the bottom.
(*7 November 1903*)

 59

Clouds of unheard-of delight—
Endless is their azure laziness.
Go away into the snowy massifs
To greet the rosy day.
Do not wake the stillness
Of the snowy hint, of tranquil thoughts…
The gently blue mountains have hidden themselves
Deep in the heavenly breast.
There till the quarrel is your all-embracing caress,
Till the war, only your tenderness;
Endless is the beginningless fairy-tale,

The birth of the sky-blue stream...
Receive the impossible delight,
O traitor! I love and summon
To greet the sky-blue lands,
The pearly waking dreams.
(*21 November 1903*)

~60~

*To M. A. Olenina-d'Alheim*[15]

A dark pale-green
Child's room.
The nanny is walking around, sleepy.
"Sleep, my little child."

In the corner is a green lamp.
It emits golden raylets of light.
The nanny is bent over the little bed...
"Let me wrap your little legs and arms."

The nanny sits down and grows pensive.
The raylets run—three raylets.
"Nanny, what are you thinking about?
Tell me about the holy martyr."

Three raylets. One is very thin...
"The holy martyr, my child, returned to God...
Close your little eyes, my sleepy little boy.
The holy martyr was freed from his suffering."
(*23 November 1903*)

15 Maria Alekseevna Olenina-d'Alheim (b. 1869) was a famous singer. Blok dedi-
cated this poem to her after he heard her sing Mussorgsky's "Child's Room."

### The Factory

In the neighboring house the windows are yellow.
In the evenings, in the evenings,
Pensive bolts creak
And people come up to the gates.

The gates are shut tight
And on the wall, on the wall,
Someone motionless and black
Is counting the people in the stillness.

I hear everything from my tower:
With a bronze voice he is calling
The people gathered below
To bend their tormented backs.

They will enter and disperse,
And hoist sacks onto their backs;
And in the yellow windows there will be laughter
About how nicely these paupers have been tricked.
(*24 November 1903*)

What ails you[16]—I do not know and will not hide
That you are ill with transparent whiteness.
Dear friend, you will find out what ails you;
You will find out next spring.

You will understand when, lying on pillows,
You will not be able to extend your arms back.
And then onto your bed will descend

---

16  Feminine in the Russian.

[ 175 ]

A continuous mournful sound.
The icon-lamp's shadow will tremble and alarm you;
Someone, separating himself from the wall,
Will approach—and slowly place over you
A gentle shroud of snowy whiteness.
(*5 December 1903*)

We were walking to the Lido at the sunrise hour
Under a net of fine rain.
You had left without giving me an answer;
I fell asleep, having gone down to the waves.

I slept restlessly, my arms spread out,
And I heard the waves' rhythmical plash.
I was beckoned by the passionate quivering of sounds
In love with the sorceress-bird.

The gull-bird, gull-maiden,
Kept descending and swimming
In the waves of the love-song
By which you lived in me.
(*11 December 1903, Petersburg*)

The fortune-teller with her wrinkled face
Was conjuring for me beneath the dark porch.
Enchanted by street shouting,
I ran after a face I had glimpsed.

I ran and guessed faces,
Stopping my running at corners.
Before me there crept a procession

Of loaded, creaking carts.
It crept like a snake between the houses—
I couldn't cross the squares…
From there came the call: "Follow us!"
And the cry: "Madman! Forgive me!"

There—tormented by an immortal will—
Perhaps You Yourself were calling…
I ran through alleys—
And was swallowed up by the houses.
(*11 December 1903*)

### 65

*To E. P. Ivanov*[17]

An infant is crying. Under the lunar sickle
A humpbacked traveler is dragging his way across the field.
In the grove someone shaggy, bent, and horned
Is laughing at the round hump.

In the field the road is pale from the moon.
Pale girls hide in the grasses.
Their hands, like the grasses, are pale and tender.
The wind rocks them left and right.

The blue stalks of grain whisper and bend.
The hunchback dances under the two-horned moon.
Someone is calling with a silvery horn.
Someone is running on the illumined road.

The pale girls got up from the grasses.
They lifted their hands toward knowledge, toward silence.
Having fallen with ear fixed to the ground,
The hunchback listens to their waiting and breathing.

17 The symbolist writer Evgeny Pavlovich Ivanov (1880–1942) was Blok's closest
friend and confidant at this time.

In the grove the shaggy figure is shivering soundlessly.
The moon has fallen into the illumined stalks.
The infant is crying. And the wind is silent.
The horn is near. And nothing can be seen in the dark.
(*14 December 1903*)

 66

Among the guests I walked in a black dress-coat.
I shook hands. Smiling, I knew:
The clock would strike. Signs would be made to me.
It would be understood that I had seen someone...

You will approach. And squeeze my hand painfully.
You will say: "You should stop it. People are laughing at you."
But I would understand—from your voice, your inflection—
That you're afraid of me more than anyone else.

Powerless and pale, I will shout
And look aimlessly around.
Then I will revive at the door with the bronze handle.
I will see everyone . . . and smile feebly.
(*18 December 1903*)

 67

*From the Newspapers*

She got up in the shining. She made the sign of the cross
Over her children and they saw a joyous dream.
Bending her head to the floor,
She made one final genuflection.

Kolya woke up. He sighed joyfully,
Still delighting in happy blue sleep.
A loud glassy sound rolled through the house and ceased:
The ringing door had slammed downstairs.
Hours passed. A man came

With a tin badge on his warm cap.
The man knocked and waited at the door.
No one opened it. They were playing hide-and-seek.

It was merry frosty Christmastide.

They were hiding Mama's red kerchief.
She used to wear it when she left in the mornings.
Today she left the kerchief at home;
The children were hiding it in the corners.

Dusk crept up on them. The children's shadows
Started leaping on the walls in the light of the street lamps.
Someone was walking up the stairs, counting the steps.
This someone finished counting. And sobbed. And knocked on the
door.

The children listened. They opened the door.
Their fat neighbor lady had brought soup.
She said: "Eat." She got down on her knees
And, bowing down like Mama, made the sign of the cross over them.

Mama doesn't feel any pain, rosy children.
Mama lay down on the rails.
Thank you, kind fat neighbor lady,
Thank you. Mama could no longer...

Mama is well. Mama died.
(*27 December 1903*)

### 68
### The Statue

The horse was being pulled by its bridle to the pig-iron
Bridge. Under the hoofs the water was black.
The horse was snorting and the moonless air
Preserved the snorting forever on the bridge.

The songs of the water and the sounds of snorting
Were diffused nearby into chaos.
They were ripped apart by invisible hands.
The reflection rushed by in the black water.

The harmonious pig-iron responded monotonously.
Difference fell away. And eternity fell asleep.
Motionlessly, bottomlessly, the black night
Carried away into the abyss the strap that had broken off.

All abided. Movement and suffering
Did not exist. The horse was snorting forever.
And on the bridle in an intensity of silence,
Hung a man eternally frozen in place.
(*28 December 1903*)

 69

A sick man was dragging himself along the shore.
Next to him crept a row of carts.

Into the smoky city a caravan was travelling
Of pretty Gypsy girls and drunken Gypsy men.

They were tossing jokes and squealing from the carts,
And next to them the man with the sack was dragging along.

He was moaning and asking that they take him to the village.
A Gypsy girl stretched out to him her swarthy arm.

And he ran up on unsteady feet
And threw his heavy bag into the cart.

His body failed; there was foam on his lips.
The girl pulled his corpse into the cart.

She sat him in the cart next to her
And the dead man kept rocking and falling on his face.

And with a song of freedom she took him to the village.
And she gave the dead husband to his wife.
(*28 December 1903*)

 70

The wind is wheezing on the bridge between the columns;
The black thread beneath the snow is humming.

Miracle is crawling beneath my sleigh,
Miracle up above is singing and singing to me...

All singing things are dolorous and difficult for me—
Your songs and the snows and the bonfires...

Miracle, I am asleep with a boundless weariness...
Miracle, lie down in the mounds of snow!
(*28 December 1903*)

71

Luminous dream, you will not deceive me:
You will lie down in the morning dew
And rise gently like red dust
On the band of sunrise.

The sun makes its circuit in the sky:
And here is evening—all afire.
A rosy sun speck is dancing
On the flowers on the wall.
On the balcony, where the mosses
Of the ancient balustrades are turning red,

The grandfathers are dozing
And dreaming of the French barricades.[18]

We listen to these ancient grandfathers
As if they were statues housed in niches:
It is sweet to remember at dinner
Old Paris in flames.

Stretching out one's ailing hand,
It is sweet to shake one's finger at the young people;
It is sweet to caress one's grandson's curls
While recounting the past.

And it is sweet to doze on the balcony
As the red sun sets,
And to sidle over to bed
In one's soft wadded robe...

They'll say: "It's late, we're tired..."
They'll withdraw at sunset,
But you and I will remain in the sitting-room
And a little sun ray will fall on the carpet.

Dear dream, evening sun ray...
Shadows of velvety eyelashes...
In the golden feathers of little clouds
The dance of tender evenings...
(*25 February 1904*)

 72

My beloved, my prince, my bridegroom,
You are sorrowful in the flowering meadow.
Like convolvulus amid the golden fields
I am twining on the other shore.

---

18 Allusion to the French revolution of 1848 in which some Russian liberals partici-
pated.

I am catching your dreams on the fly
Like a pale-white transparent flower;
You will trample me in full flower
With your weary white-chested horse.

Ah, even if you trample my immortality,
I will preserve the fire for you.
Timidly, I will light the flame
Of the church candle at the pale matins.

In the church you will stand, pale of face,
And come to the empress of heaven—
I will quiver like the waxy flame
And make you feel the familiar shiver...

Above you—like a candle—I am gentle;
Before you—like a flower—I am tender.
I await you, my bridegroom:
All bride—and eternally wife.
(*26 March 1904*)

🌿73🌿

*Prayers*
Our Argo!
(Andrey Bely)[19]

I.

Faithful servants, we stand guard
    At the entrance to the tower.
We believe passionately, measure the heights,
    And eternally await the horn.
Eternally means tomorrow. At the grating
    Every day and hour
Is praised by the clear voice
    Of one of us.

---

19 The epigraph is taken from Bely's poem "The Golden Fleece." Bely had orga-
nized a group of young Moscow symbolist poets called the Argonauts.

The air is full of deep sighs,
   Of stormy hopes.
The heights burn from the unclosing
   Of enflamed eyelids.

The rose angel will point
   And say: "Here she is:
Beads are being threaded, are being woven into threads
   By Eternal Spring."

At a radiant moment we will hear the sounds
   Of receding storms.
We will silently tie our hands together
   And fly into the azure.

2.

*Morning Prayer*

Till morning we argue in the rooms;
At sunrise one of us
Goes out to the rose light—
To greet the golden hour.

He stands high above us,
His thin profile against the pale dawn.
Behind his shoulders, behind his shoulders
All the fields and forests are in silver.

And so he stands in a silvery circle,
Majestic, merciful, and stern.
On his pale pure brow
We read that the time is at hand.

3.

*Evening Prayer*

The sun descends to the west. Silence.
My vanity slumbers.
The breathing of those around me is rhythmical.
Before me the horizon is on fire.

I call you, mortal comrade!
Come out! Move apart, earth!
On the ashes of fires that have roared through,
I stand, having satisfied my life.

Come, confess my sleepiness,
Give me communion and wipe my lips…
Satisfy me with the quiet victory
Of the red flaming sunset.

4.
*Night Prayer*
They see Her!
(V. Briusov)[20]

To You, Whose Darkness was so bright,
Whose Voice calls with quietude—
Raise the ever sagging vault
Of the heavenly arches.
My hour of prayer is not long—
As morning approaches, sleep will possess me.
There still rings in my soul a splinter
Of past and future times.
And in this hour, which is brief,
I call with my tormented soul:
Come! Prolong the remainder
Of moments glimpsed in waking reality.
To You, Whose Shadow long trembles
In the rosy sunset dust!
Before Whom agonizes and gnashes his teeth
The stern magician of my land!
To You, the Banner of the last tribes,
You, the Resurrecting Shadow!
I call You! Incline over us!
Clothe us in Your vestment of quietude!

20  Blok's poem is a response to Briusov's anti-sophianic polemical poem "To the
Younger Poets" ("They see Her! They hear Her!…"). Briusov was called a "magician"
by himself and others.

5.
*Night Prayer*

Sleep. Let your sleep be tranquil.
I pray. I listen to your breathing.
I sorrow like a celestial warrior
Whose armor has fallen to earth.

Infinitely light is my burden.
Only these moments are heavy.
Everything will be swept away by the golden time:
My chains, thoughts, and books.

One who rebels, has a generous heart,
But infinitely right is one who is silent.
I am in anguish beneath a cedar of Lebanon,
You, in the shade of a peaceful olive tree.

I am a madman! My heart has been stabbed
By the red coal of the prophet!
The branches of peace overshadow you...
 Unwakeable girl... Sleep until it's time.
(March–April 1904)

 74

The distances are blind, the days are without wrath,
    The lips are closed.
In the Tsarevna's[21] deep sleep
    The blueness is empty.

There were days when above the towers
    The sunset was aflame.
Gently, with white words
    Brother called out to brother.

---

21  See footnote 6 on p. 143.

From distant cells brother to brother
    Proclaimed: "Praise!"
Somewhere the doves cooed,
    Fluttering their wings.

From their golden hives the bees
    Brought honey.
The festive people filled the valleys
    With merriment.

In colored beads, in red ribbons,
    Girls bloomed...
Who is galloping there adorned with galloons
    In the blue dust?

A rider in fine attire,
    In golden brocade.
With luminous curls on his head
    And sparks on his sword.

His horse white as cherry blossom...
    The stirrups glitter...
Spring has poured itself out
    On his brocade caftan.

Poured itself out—he vanishes in the clouds
    To reappear, glistening, beyond the hill.
He rises on the green cliffs
    In the light of dawn.

His feathers quiver and he
    Shouts: "Beware!"
He dances through the village on his horse
    And at night he disappears in the heights...

At night the girls dream of him:
    He flies down from the clouds;
The horse is like a flash of lightning,
    The rider is like a fleeting ray of light...

And like a ray he passes into the coolness
    Of the narrow window,
And the Tsarevna, happy to receive a guest,
    Rises from her bed of sleep...

Or, in cruel days of foul weather,
    She looks into the sleepy pond
And, trembling with passion,
    His arms entwine her.

But then his arms deceive her,
    Thrusting her
Toward the silver,
    Pushing her into the streamy game...

And her soul, flying north
    Like a golden bee,
Into a red dream, into honeyed clover,
    Lies down for its repose...

And again in wreaths and dews
    The dream sings
And the gold of his shield
    Glistens on the cliffs.

The maiden picks up the shield
    And again in the distance
The rider rises, the horse rears
    In the blue dust...

There will be an eternal change of springs
    And the yoke of downfalls.
A whirlwind full of visions—
    A flight of doves...

What is momentary powerlessness?
   Time is light smoke...
We will again stretch our wings
   And fly off anew!

And again, in insane change
   Cutting through the firmament,
We will encounter a new whirlwind of visions,
   We will encounter life and death!
(*22 April–20 May 1904, Shakhmatovo*)

In the hour when narcissuses get drunk
And the theater is bathed in sunset fire,
In the semi-shadow of the final stage-wings
Someone is walking and sighing over me...

Is it Harlequin who has forgotten about his role?
Or you, my quiet-eyed doe?
Or the gentle wind, bringing from the field
A light tribute of breezes?

I, a clown, at the lighted front edge of the stage,
Emerge through an open trap-door.
This is the abyss that looks through the lamps—
An insatiably greedy spider.

And while the narcissuses get drunk,
I play the fool, spinning and ringing...
But in the shadow of the final stage-wings
Someone is weeping out of pity for me.

The tender friend with the blue mist
Is rocked by the lullaby swing of dreams.
Nestling like an orphan close to my wounds
Is the light-fingered fragrance of flowers.
(*26 May 1904, Shakhmatovo*)

Here it is-the series of steps ascending to your grave.
There is no one else here. We are alone.
Sleep, tender companion of days
Flooded with unprecedented light.

You are reposing in your white grave.
You call out with a smile: do not wake me.
Golden locks on your brow,
A golden icon on your breast.

I celebrated your radiant death
By touching my lips to your waxy hand;
The rest is preserved by the bottomless
Firmament in blue darkness.

Sleep-no one will interrupt your repose.
We are at the edge of unknown roads.
The whole stormy night
Your radiant palace shines forth.
(*18 June 1904, Shakhmatovo*)

Made in the USA
Lexington, KY
23 April 2019